LIVE
life

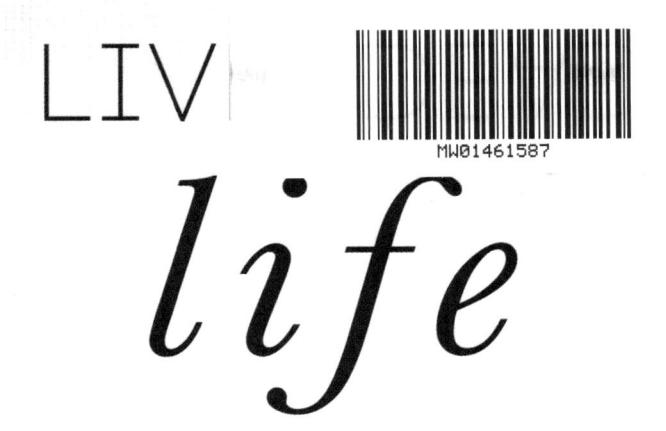

FOLLOWING *Jesus* OUTSIDE MY DOOR

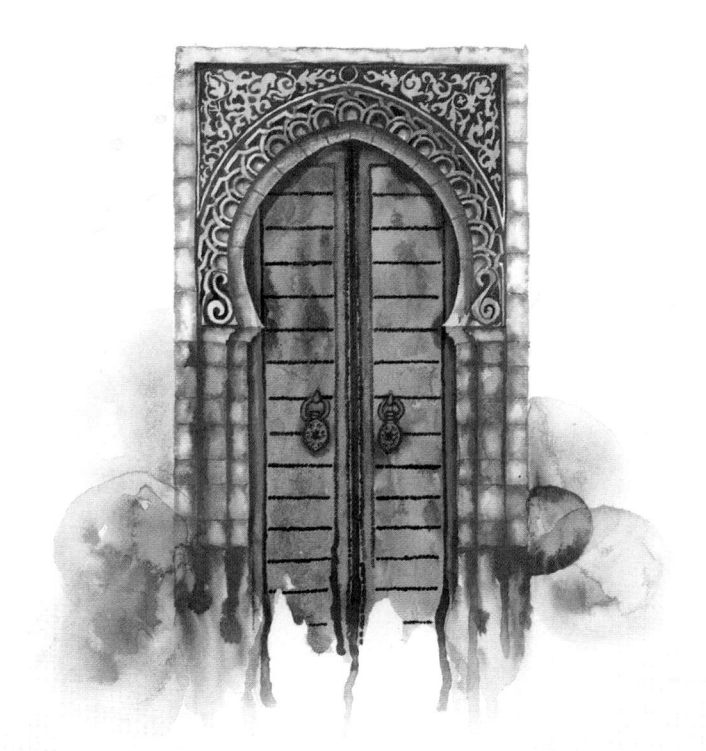

A 30-DAY DEVOTIONAL FOR YOUTH
Written by Joy Hawthorne

Copyright © 2017 Live Dead.
ALL RIGHTS RESERVED.

Published by Abide Publishers LLC
1600 N. Boonville, Suite B&C, Springfield, MO 65803

Cover design, typesetting, and interior design by Lucent Digital (lucentdigital.co).

No portion of this book may be reproduced, stored in a retrieval system, ortransmitted in any form or by any means—electronic, mechanical, photocopy,recording, or any other—except for brief quotations in printed reviews, withoutthe prior written permission of the publisher.

Unless otherwise specified, Scripture quotations used in this book are fromThe New King James Version®. Copyright © 1982 by Thomas Nelson, Inc. Used by permission. All rights reserved.

Cover and interior artwork by Danielle Hartzler

ISBN: 978-0-9981789-2-9
Printed in the United States of America

Contents

5	INTRODUCTION
8	ABIDE
10	DAY 1: ADMIT THE MESS
14	DAY 2: MY STICKY NOTE BRAIN
18	DAY 3: LIFE REVOLVES AROUND THE SON
22	DAY 4: CALL AND RESPONSE
26	DAY 5: BRICKS AND MORE BRICKS
30	DAY 6: GET OUT, DOUBT!
34	DAY 7: ALL IS NOT LOST
38	DAY 8: THERE'S ALWAYS MORE TO LEARN
42	DAY 9: BE GRATEFUL FOR YOUR FREE REFILLS
46	DAY 10: MORE THAN ONCE
54	APOSTLE
56	DAY 11: YOU'RE INVITED
60	DAY 12: HIS HEARTBEAT
64	DAY 13: SOMEBODY'S WATCHING ME
68	DAY 14: SCOURING THE LAND
72	DAY 15: ADVENTURE TIME
76	DAY 16: A VOICE: WE ALL HAVE ONE
80	DAY 17: WAITING FOR MY SHOES
84	DAY 18: MY STRENGTHENING LOVE
88	DAY 19: IT TAKES A VILLAGE
92	DAY 20: TOGETHER
100	ABANDON
102	DAY 21: THIS IS HOME
106	DAY 22: CROSS BEARING
110	DAY 23: NO RISK IS TOO GREAT
114	DAY 24: FACE THE DANGER
118	DAY 25: THE SEE-THROUGH ME IS FREE
122	DAY 26: NOW THAT YOU KNOW
126	DAY 27: COME SIT WITH US
130	DAY 28: THE LITTLE RED HEART
134	DAY 29: DANCING REQUIRED
140	DAY 10: I SEEK APPROVAL
145	A PRAYER

INTRODUCTION

"It's a dangerous business, Frodo, going out your door. You step on the road, and if you don't keep your feet, there's no knowing where you might be swept off to."

– J. R. R. TOLKIEN, "THE LORD OF THE RINGS"

This is a snapshot of my abiding in Jesus for thirty days while living in North Africa. There were good days, bad days, and days that were just days as I wrote about what it means for me to die daily and live for Jesus in Libya.

I'm not that much further along the journey than many of you are, and what I share in these pages are things I'm definitely still learning. I simply want to show how I choose to follow Jesus as I step outside my door each day.

I'm in the middle of a crazy, joyful, hard life, a life with Jesus. I'm committed and excited about going deeper with Him. I step outside my door and follow Jesus where He leads. I seek to keep my feet on the path with Jesus, knowing a great adventure waits. I would love for you to join me.

HOW TO GET THE MOST OUT OF THIS BOOK

We make time for what matters to us. Set aside time each day for just you and Jesus. Read the daily Scripture passages included: one chapter from the Old Testament, one Psalm, one Gospel chapter, and one chapter from Acts or the Epistles. Each day's Scriptures complement the day's journal entry.

After reading each entry, take time to reflect on it, using the questions included. As you read through them, record your answers. Be honest. Search yourself. Ask hard questions. Stretch yourself, and go a little deeper. Don't rush through it. Ask God to speak, and wait for His answer.

Each entry also includes a few suggested worship songs to use in your abiding time. You can use the songs to start or end your abiding time. Use them as prayers during your prayer time. You will find complete playlists on Spotify and YouTube by searching for LiveDeadSpeak.

Join the conversation with me and other readers by sharing your thoughts using #livedead on Instagram, Twitter, or Facebook.

الثبات

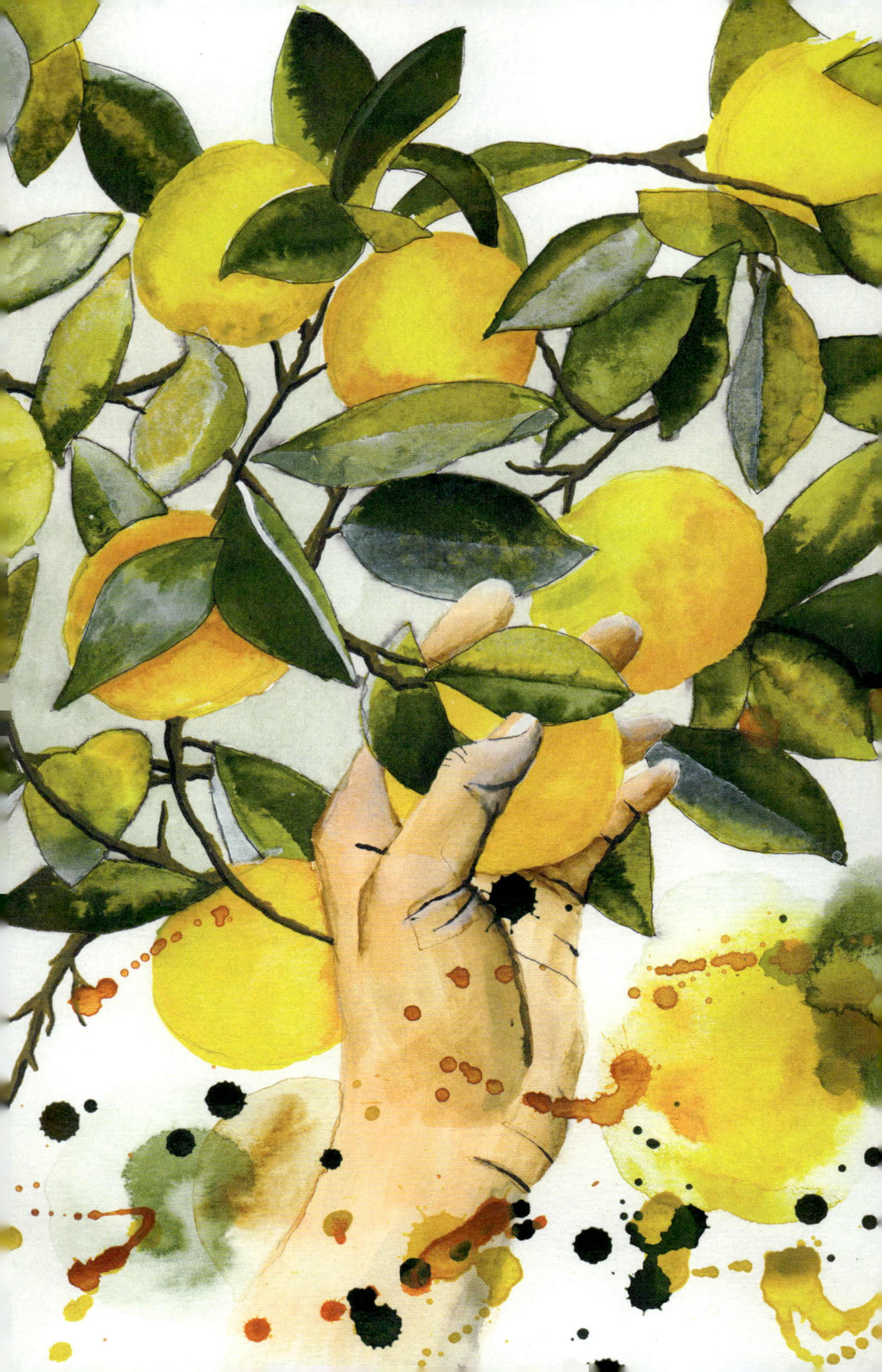

Abide

ABIDING
CHARACTER
SPIRIT EMPOWERMENT
LIFELONG LEARNING

In this first section, my journal entries center on our core value of Abide. Abiding simply means to be our best for Jesus. It took a few years of being a missionary kid to better understand what all these values really meant for my daily life. Below are my thoughts on what I thought these words meant. Take a few minutes to write your own definitions.

ABIDING:

I had not heard the word "abide" before Live Dead, but my family has been with Live Dead since I was little. Abiding has been a part of my vocabulary for as long as I can remember. "Abide," they said, in every conversation and sermon. That said, when I thought about abiding, I thought about spending time with Jesus for a few quick minutes in the morning.

I define abiding as:

CHARACTER:

I defined character as who I am on the inside or what I'm made of. Character determined if I was a good person or not. It was either something people had or didn't have.

I define character as:

SPIRIT EMPOWERMENT:

I thought this meant big things like physical healings and miracles or people falling on their knees. Spirit empowerment was someone with a powerful voice booming, preaching to the multitudes with lots of eloquent words and immediate, convincing results. I didn't know how Spirit empowerment would look or work coming through me.

I define Spirit empowerment as:

LIFELONG LEARNING:

Whenever I thought of learning, all that came to mind was school and language learning. To be a good learner was to work hard.

I define lifelong learning as:

DAY 1

Admit the Mess
2 Chronicles 29; Psalm 23; John 15; Romans 5

Clutter frustrates me. Yet I have clothes piled around my room, books and papers all over my desk, and stacks of just stuff everywhere in my bedroom because I get lazy or busy. "I'll take care of that later when I have more time," I often hear myself saying. I wish I could say it's a battle I try to win, but alas, I rarely want to fight the battle. Eventually the clutter builds until it breaks me, and in that moment, I have to admit that yes, my room is a mess, and I have to clean it.

My room and my life can be a lot alike. Things start out pretty orderly, usually around New Year's, and I have a new calendar and a schedule. I start my day with abiding time, move on to school, and so forth. That is until an unexpected guest drops by, there's a last-minute meeting, my homework takes too long or I go to bed too late, and I wake up the next morning and just want to sleep. So I do, until it's time for school. Let this go on for a day or two or more, and suddenly everything is out of whack. My perfectly situated schedule is gone. And eventually, just like my room, I need to admit the mess and do something about it because the busyness of life overtook my priorities.

So I stop and invite Jesus in. I gather up the piles of guilt and laziness and hand them over. I take a moment (or several moments) and give the messiness to Him. I decide to not let the busyness of life and my long to-do list clutter my way to Jesus anymore. There is always something to be done, some big or little distraction that would take me from my abiding time. Some reasons are legitimate—but some are just not. And if I let one thing slip into the schedule, then a second can easily follow, and before I know it, I can't see the floor of my bedroom, and the clutter pushes Jesus to the bottom of the to-do list.

I know the importance and the impact of abiding time on my life and on the work we do here. I know that I need to talk to Jesus, to listen to Him and praise Him. I know I need to spend time thanking Him. And I need to do it *especially when* I don't feel like it or I don't feel like I have the time because it's in those moments that the clutter starts to build, when I let something take the first place before Jesus. Jesus is my desire. He is my delight. I believe that. Jesus deserves to be number one on my list. So while my life and schedule can be busy and while it is a big choice to stop and not do anything else before time with Him, He is worth that choice.

Jesus invites me to the table where He is everything—the bread of life and the living water. He invites me to stop for a few moments to talk, laugh, and cry. He always has something to say or something to show me. How much love and life do I miss because I'm too busy to stop and enjoy time with Jesus? When I'm with a friend, I don't leave the room to work on another project. I stay and hang out with her. And I don't ever leave my friend sitting in the chair in my room with clothes and books piling up on top of her. So if Jesus is my friend and if He is truly worth everything, why do I leave the room to do something else and let my schoolwork and language school and social time pile up on top of Him?

It might be easier to say yes to Jesus in a church service or prayer meeting, but does it count more to say yes to Him when I am busy with school, when I'm tired, or when I'm just plain bored? There are times I wish all the things I do for Jesus as a missionary kid should count towards my quiet, personal time with Him, but abiding isn't about checking something off the missions checklist. Jesus needs to have priority in my schedule if He is to have priority in my life. To go through my day *for* Jesus, I need to spend time *with* Him. I can only give *for* Jesus of what I received *from* Him. That is why I need time with Him daily.

Jesus wants me to cross the line from responsibility to relationship. He desires me to say that I *want* to abide in Him, not I *have* to abide in Him. At the end of the day (and at the end of time for that matter), it'll be about who I am, not what I did. To become who I am in Jesus, I need to spend time with Him regularly. I've discovered that as I carve out time for Him, He carves Himself into me. The time I spend with Him is never a waste and it never leads to clutter.

Abide in Him

It's time to admit the mess. What clutter or distractions keep you from abiding with Jesus?

If your distractions are physical items, pick them up right now and make the motion of handing them to Jesus. If your clutter is thoughts or memories, gather them up and write them down, then make the motion of handing them to Jesus. Out loud, ask Jesus to take these and hold them for you and then thank Him with your own words of praise.

Are you willing to change your schedule so that Jesus has the best of your time every day? If yes, write down what your schedule needs to look like.

To make a daily commitment, you may need someone to hold you accountable, someone to encourage and remind you of the reason why you want more of Jesus in your life. Who is that person? Talk to him or her today when your abiding time is finished.

SONGS FOR ABIDING:
"Running in Circles" (United Pursuit); "Nothing Is Wasted" (Elevation Worship); "Abide With Me" (Audrey Assad)

I LOVE BEING A MISSIONARY KID BECAUSE

Being a missionary kid is an amazing experience. You get to experience different cultures and do things that others might not normally do. You get to make new friends and best of all, share the word of Jesus to those who desperately need it.

LOGAN
North Africa
Age 17

"I know that I need to talk to Jesus, to listen to Him and praise Him."

DAY 2

My Sticky Note Brain
Isaiah 40; Psalm 24; Luke 10; Philippians 4

I hate it when the electricity goes out—especially in the summer. "Noooooo," I groan because I know that in minutes I'm going to feel like I'm dying. It's the hardest thing about living here—sometimes the electricity is out for eight hours or longer. Thankfully, unlike our electricity, God's power never shuts off. But the trick is to stay connected to Him, the source, in order to receive power from Him, to receive His life. If I'm not connected, I can't receive the power.

So, I have my abiding time in the morning. I beat the clutter monster in my life and it's great. But what happens after I finish that time with Jesus? Because I find it real easy to just start going about my business and forget everything I just talked to Jesus about. How easy it can be for Jesus to slip from my mind. How do I walk with Him all day? How do I stay connected to His awesome power?

I discovered that it's easier to walk with Jesus all day when I think of Him as a friend I live with and not as a duty I spend time with. When I intentionally involve God in all areas of my life throughout the day, even the small, seemingly unimportant things, I remember that He's there and that He cares and understand—because, like a friend, what happens to me in a day matters to Him. He knows what's going on in my life, but so often I just forget to ask for help, and I've found that a quick prayer in the moment or quick word of thanks makes Him feel close.

One other thing that helps me to remember Him all day: sticky notes. I stick notes around me to remind me throughout the day where it all began. They remind me of Jesus and His gifts to me. I see little verses and song lyrics all around me. I think God is OK with me and my sticky note brain.

I don't believe that I can just check in with God. I don't send a message to update Him about where I am. He's always present. He's always here, waiting, speaking, and listening. But I also found that breaks throughout the day help me spend time with Him, so I set aside a few times where I can sit in my bedroom or go up to the little room on our roof that overlooks the city and pray or journal or just sit. With practice it gets much easier to spend time with Jesus. It takes a lot of practice to intentionally involve Him in all part of my day, and I often forget, but I keep trying. And maybe that's what Jesus wants—not perfection in a moment but persistence over time.

What Jesus really wants is just me. I used to make homemade gifts for my dad when I was little. You know, some real Picasso-like artwork made from construction paper and glitter and glue. My dad always appreciated those, mostly because he loved me and not because I was some protégé artist. The same goes for God. He appreciates my gifts and the work I've done in a day, but what He really wants is just me, my love, my worship, and my time, and not all the pretty things I can create for Him. He wants me to enjoy Him, rather than rushing out to do something for Him.

Jesus says, "Remain in Me." Without Jesus, I have no power or life. I become a dry and withered branch, and I don't want to live like that. My set abiding time and the rest of my day are not two totally separate things because Jesus is the same always. He is the Vine all day, and I trust Him to take care of me and to point me in the right direction, but I must stay connected. I must remain in Him. Though I abide in Jesus all day, I have no guarantee that everything will work out perfectly or that every person I talk to will accept the gospel, but I do have the guarantee that I will always have life. Philippians 4:13 says: "I can do all things through Christ who strengthens me." Abiding is the power. It's my connection, my hand to hold, and the Father that never lets go. I get my strength for life by walking with Jesus all day.

MY STICKY NOTE BRAIN

Abide in Him

Abiding takes intentionality. It takes practice. Sometimes it takes sticky notes. What is your sticky note? What tools can you use to remind you of the presence of Jesus all day?

Do you ever talk to yourself? Direct that conversation to Jesus instead. What if Jesus became your new best "imaginary friend"? Try it out right now. Have a conversation with Jesus about normal life activities.

Take this challenge: Remember Jesus all day long today. Write out three notes with a favorite lyric from a worship song along with a Scripture verse. Put them in places that you know you will see them throughout the day—the back of your phone, in your locker, in a binder, or on a mirror. As Jesus becomes part of your everyday activities, you will experience fullness. His strength will empower you to face anything that your day may bring.

SONGS FOR ABIDING:
"May God Be Everywhere I Go" (Mosaic MSC); "All I Need Is In You" (Emmanuel LIVE); "I Need Thee Every Hour" (Anthem Lights)

LIVING IN MY COUNTRY IS DIFFICULT BECAUSE

Being a missionary kid, where I live is difficult because you can't call yourself a missionary. You have to be a businessperson or a language teacher or something acceptable in this society. It's also hard because the devil doesn't want us here. He throws obstacles at us left and right and is constantly trying to discourage us.

J. E.
North Africa
Age 17

"I get my strength for life by walking with Jesus all day."

DAY 3

Life Revolves Around the Son

Genesis 1; Psalm 34; John 3; Ephesians 1

In the beginning, creation reflected God and His glory. I imagine His laughter in the flowers and His strength in the lion. I see His strokes of harmonious colors in the sunset. I hear freedom flowing in the sparkling water of a river. All of creation pointed to the Source. When He made humans, He made us in His own image—to reflect Him in what we do and through who we are, in the way we smile and laugh, in how we interact with others, in how we love and in how we live. His light shines in us to affect everything and everyone around us. We are designed to reflect His image to the world.

To reflect the image of God to the world, I have to know what He looks like and sounds like, right? I can't do that without spending time with Him, and so it's through my abiding time that I see Jesus and know Him and hear His voice. As I spend time with Him, I get a picture of Him to reflect to others. Jesus in me naturally flows out of me. Abiding affects everything and everyone around me.

I want to grow closer to God, but I'll admit there are days that it sounds like too much work, and there are days that I miss my abiding time. It can be easy to give up and skip it. But I know, I have felt and experienced, that to grow closer to Jesus is a daily choice to follow Him. I become more like God by living my life daily with Jesus. I bring Him my problems and fears, my joy and sadness, and hand them all to Jesus. I put Him at the center and give Him all. My life reflects what is at the center. I imagine it to be something like a solar system. The center is a sun, and all parts of my life revolve around it. Jesus is the sun; He is the center. My life revolves around Him, and His light shines through me to the world beyond. Abiding keeps the sun bright, keeps Jesus at the center. It keeps my eyes on Jesus and no one or nothing else.

In John 3, the people John the Baptist baptized started following Jesus, and John's disciples were jealous for him. They worried about his popularity. John, on the other hand, wasn't upset; he was pleased! He saw himself as a friend, a stepping-stone to Jesus. "He must become greater, and I must become less," he said. This doesn't mean I can make God any greater than He already is. It means I make much of God in my life and less of me. He becomes more visible, and I fade into the background. He is what my story is about. That doesn't mean that I don't matter; it just means that I make the choice to lift Jesus higher, that Jesus is the One I praise, that Jesus is who I live for. I give Jesus not only first place—I give Him the only place. When He shines from the center of my life, then that is what people see.

When I abide in Jesus, people see more of Him and less of me. A heart full of Jesus leaves no room for me. "It is in Christ we find who we are and what we are living for" (Eph. 1:11 MSG). With abiding at the center, my life becomes like John the Baptist's life. I can be a voice in the desert and a friend of Jesus that invites others to know Him. With Jesus at the center of my life, I reflect Him. On good days and bad days, I find His praise is ever on my lips (Ps. 34:1).

Abide in Him

When people meet you, what do you want them to remember? Pray that they would leave knowing that you love Jesus.

A lifestyle of thanksgiving removes selfishness from our hearts. As we thank Jesus for all He gives us, we learn that He never leaves us. Praising Jesus in midst of bad days teaches you to fight the right way. Praise and thanksgiving will bring you closer to Him. "From my heart to the heavens, Jesus, be the center. It's all about you. Yes, it's all about you."

Are you experiencing any fears or problems right now? Take a few moments to simply praise Him as you ask God to teach you to trust Him more as He walks beside you.

What are you thankful for today? Take a few moments to thank Jesus for all He has done for you.

SONGS FOR ABIDING:
"Shine on Us" (William Matthews, Bethel); "Jesus at the Center" (Israel & New Breed); "Ever Be" (Kalley Heiligenthal, Bethel Music)

ONE THING JESUS HAS TAUGHT ME ABOUT MISSIONS IS

You should be prepared to face criticism for your beliefs. Jesus said we would be hated because of Him. Almost every time I go to a park, a boy will be rude to my family and me because of the cross I wear on my neck.

ABRAM
North Africa
Age 13

"I give Jesus not only first place—I give Him the only place."

DAY 4

Call and Response
Genesis 40; Psalm 19; John 21; 2 Timothy 1

My older brother goes to boarding school, and another girl my age just started there as well. People ask if I'm going to go, too. The answer as I see it today is no. God asked me to let my little light shine for Him here. I tell everyone in all honesty that I love the people here, and I'm happy here. Libya is just stuck with me.

Sometimes I think it'd be nice to go to boarding school and live in that environment. There are things I miss that I can't get here—like American candy, free soda refills, and Christian friends. There aren't many Christian teenagers around here. I don't feel deprived because God gives me what I need every day, and I trust Him to always provide, to fill in those gaps.

You see, God called my parents to Libya—but He also called me. Some missionary kids feel like God calls their parents so they're just along for the ride. But I believe God calls the kids as much as the parents. Sure, I didn't choose this life to begin with; I was 15 months old the first time we moved overseas. So, God has spoken to me differently than He spoke to my parents. I didn't pick this place, but I can decide how I'm going to live here.

And how do I know God wants me (and my family) here? First, we were kicked out of our previous country and couldn't return, so we started searching for the next location that God had in mind for us. Several places came up, but nothing seemed right. When Libya was suggested, we all felt a collective yes. We visited as a family and then prepared to move. Second, in the process of moving, God spoke to me and touched my heart and stirred something in me that I never had before—love, overwhelming love for the needs here. There are so many unreached people around us. I don't think I could've felt such love for a place and a people without God speaking to me.

I know God wants to speak to me and guide me, and there are a few ways that He does this.

The Bible: I get God's instructions from His Word. The Bible is real and alive.

Other People: He speaks through other people, either through prayer or testimony or encouraging words. I have had people I trust share a word or a picture with me at just the moment that I needed it. God uses these people to encourage, direct, and rebuke me.

Prayer: He also speaks through prayer or times of silence. Sometimes in prayer, God brings a need or country or person for whom to pray.

Dreams: He can also use dreams in which He shares a need or call, like He did with Paul in his vision on the road to Damascus.

Circumstances: God also uses our circumstances, like He did when the country we lived in closed to us. God uses these situations to point us in a different direction. He opens and shuts doors.

Nature: Psalm 19:1 says, "The heavens proclaim the glory of God. The skies display his craftsmanship." God uses nature to proclaim His glory and to speak to us.

These are just some of the ways that I hear God's voice, ways that He shares things with me. But what happens after I hear a word from Him or He puts a call on my heart? What is my response? The response is as important as the actual hearing.

For me, God put the need of unreached people on my heart. He put Libya on my heart. And once we arrived in the country, it wasn't hard to find the need. All I had to do was look around. I might not be perfect, but I can follow Jesus and be there for them. I can be their first Christian friend. I can live with them. I can share my heart and the gospel with them. All I have to do is say, "Yes." Yes to whatever Jesus has for me and wherever He wants to take me, whether I feel ready or not. A pastor from India once told me, "God does not call the qualified; He qualifies the called." Sometimes I feel unworthy of the call. I think there are way more talented, experienced, and qualified people to do this. But God didn't ask them, He asked me. In the moment He asks, my best choice is to follow Him.

CALL AND RESPONSE

Abide in Him

Create your own list, like the one above, of the ways in which God speaks to you.

Today, as you pass people, ask yourself if your heart breaks for them. Do the lost have your heart? Pray that God would give you a deeper burden for the lost all across the world.

Has there been a circumstance in your life that was difficult, but then something good came out of it? Be willing to trust that God is always in control. As you seek Him, He will speak through dreams, pictures, and other people. What words or pictures is God showing you, and what is your response to them? Speak them out to Jesus, and write them down.

SONGS FOR ABIDING:
"Closer" (Steffany Gretzinger, Bethel Music); "Impossible" (Meredith Andrews); "Turn Your Eyes Upon Jesus" (Hillsong Worship)

JESUS IS WORTH LIVING FOR BECAUSE

He is good.

PAXTON
Middle East
Age 8

LIVE DEAD LIFE

"I know God wants to speak to me and guide me…"

DAY 5

Bricks and More Bricks

Proverbs 1; Psalm 139; Matthew 7; 2 Corinthians 3

I want to be a person of good character. I'm just not sure I want to do all the work to get it. I want the destination—but I'd rather take a heavenly elevator to get there instead of the long road. People of character, those all-out followers of Jesus that I admire so much, are not born that way—they become that way through a life lived for Jesus.

I can make the choice to do the same every day. Building character is work, and often it's hard work. I imagine it to be like building a house, brick by brick, but the house is never really finished—I just keep adding on rooms. Character develops inside me, brick by brick, as I follow Jesus day by day.

I ask myself, "How do I build a wall that lasts or build character that lasts?" Well, first, I have to be intentional. I have to decide to do it. Just like abiding, I have to make the decision. Done. I want to be a person of good character. Next, I need a foundation for the walls of bricks. That foundation is Jesus. My character is built on Jesus. It's built in my abiding time, in time spent with Jesus. I spend time with Jesus today and listen to what He asks me to do. When I choose to do what God asks, when I choose to obey Him, I place a brick in the building of my character. When I choose to not obey God, I leave something out of my character, and it weakens it. It's like a part of the wall is missing. So, time with Jesus is necessary, and obedience to His voice is necessary.

Building character is a journey, not a destination. It will take resolve, motivation, and strength in Jesus. I need focus and determination to cross the finish line. I can't second guess or dwell in the past. I need to fix my eyes ahead on Jesus and keep moving forward. It's likely that I will trip along the way. No matter if I catch myself or fall flat on my face, I got to get back up and start running again, and as I continue saying "yes" to God, the bricks keep stacking up. (Is it weird to have a running and brick-laying metaphor smashed together? Probably. Oh well. You get the idea.)

Building a life of good character means making the right choices now. It means choosing to invest time in a relationship with Jesus. Abiding in Him builds something that lasts. The time investment works itself out in my character. God uses it to make who I am in Him. I start today by listening to Him and saying yes and making the choices that match His character. So today I commit to building my character—in my daily habits and in the unexpected circumstances. I choose to respond with a yes. An immediate yes does not always come naturally to me, but I can choose today to say yes immediately and then follow through on it. In the end, the evidence will be in what we did and in who we are. Character will show in what we did, not only in the big decisions, but in the seemingly small ones, when no one was watching, when it was hard.

Character becomes my strength. These bricks of my life on a foundation of Jesus are like a fortress. I remember the three little pigs: one made a house of straw, another of sticks, and the third of brick. When the wolf huffed and puffed, the only house that stood was the one made of brick. (Looks like I'm onto something in this character building analogy!) The strength of my character comes from my foundation—and my foundation is Jesus, so that's pretty strong. If I build my character on myself, if I build my character on my talents and skills, if I build my character on my choices for the future, then what have I built? Not anything that will last. In the flesh, I am a temporal being. To build something that last for eternity takes building on Someone who knows eternity. I want to build a life of good character from now into eternity. Which means I need to give up the quick fixes and do the hard work. Which means I need to abide in Jesus and do whatever He asks.

The house never takes the credit for itself. The beauty of the house points to the builder. And I choose Jesus as my builder.

Abide in Him

Make an honest assessment of your character. What does your reputation say about your character today?

In what areas of your life do you feel like your character is weak—where what you say doesn't match with who you are? At school, work, church? With family, friends, Jesus?

Do you want to be a person of good character? Make the determination today. When God prompts you to do something, say yes and follow through right away. Write down those moments, and make them markers so you can see where the bricks were laid.

A daily choice to be like Jesus takes complete surrender. The more you pray and seek to live a life of good character, the more you see the things that Jesus is asking you to get rid of. The process of becoming more like Jesus is never easy, but it sure is worth it. Are you willing today to build a strong foundation in the Lord? Write out a prayer and share where you are and where you would like to be.

SONGS FOR ABIDING:
"Everything and Nothing Less" (Chris McClarney, Jesus Culture); "Glory to Glory" (William Matthews, Bethel Music); "Let Them See You" (Colton Dixon)

JESUS IS WORTH DYING FOR BECAUSE

He died for us! And when we go to heaven, we get to be with Him!

BENJAMIN
North Africa
Age 10

"Building character is a journey, not a destination."

DAY 6

Get Out, Doubt!

Exodus 3; Psalm 77; John 20; Galatians 5

Sometimes doubt creeps in. I really believe God can and will use me to reach the unreached people around me, but sometimes I ask, "How is this possible?" One little me surrounded by lots of needs.

When there are a lot of questions and very few answers, it feels like doubt has moved in, unpacked its suitcase, and claimed my bed. The doubt starts whispering in my ear about what God can and cannot do with me. But when I push back and throw doubt's belongings out of my room, when I believe that God can do His big things with little me, that's when tiny me turns into a mountain mover. When I see beyond myself and beyond my doubt to an empty grave and scars that save, I believe in God's power to fulfill His promises. As I push doubt out the door, I invite God in to work and move.

This giant need in Libya all depends on God coming down and working. I am nothing without God, and I depend on His Spirit to empower me. When my mom and I visit the ladies in our neighborhood, I pray that the Holy Spirit would fill the atmosphere and direct my words. I'm pretty shy and don't easily jump into conversations. I like to take my time to think things through. But when it's lively conversation over tea, I have to make the choice to speak up. Sometimes it's a big leap of faith for me—what if I say the wrong thing or what if they don't respond positively? I don't want to look bad. But the alternative of not saying any of the words that I prayed the Holy Spirit would give me, that's not an option either. So I ask the Holy Spirit to move, and I choose to believe in the power of God. I choose to die to myself and live for Jesus. In that moment, the Holy Spirit moves.

I always want to be ready when God speaks. All doubts pushed aside. I trust the Holy Spirit inside me. I'll take the step for God's glory and power to be displayed. I might not see how God will move, but I'll be ready to follow His Spirit no matter what. I truly desire to live with the Holy Spirit flowing through me. Of course, when I say that I'm ready to go when God speaks doesn't mean I have it all together. It just means I'm willing to do whatever God asks me to do, believing that He uses broken people like me.

So to be ready for all this I seek the fruits of the Holy Spirit. He empowers me with love, joy, peace, patience, kindness, goodness, gentleness, faithfulness, and self-control. So often I read the fruits of the Spirit as a list of things I need to be, but it's not the fruit of me—it's the fruit of the Spirit. The fruits of the Holy Spirit are alive and move through me. The Spirit is the source of my living dead, and I choose to believe the Holy Spirit in me is going to meet the big need through little me.

Now I like a good plan. I like to know the details of what's happening, and our team has a strategy for reaching the lost and planting the church here. It's not like we don't have a plan, but our strategy should never be a substitute for the Holy Spirit. Because some things I just can't force. I can't make the perfect encounter with a Libyan teenage girl happen. I can't change her heart. I have to rely on God for that. That's the work of the Holy Spirit. I can help set the stage but God must show up for the show. I speak and I love and I trust that God has prepared the soil of their hearts. I can plant the seed, but God is the harvester.

Abide in Him

Do you ever have moments in which you want to say or do something, but then doubt creeps in, so you stop? Today, believe that you are never alone. God is with you and the Holy Spirit lives inside you. Follow His prompts.

How do you see the fruits of the Spirit work through you? Look inward and consider how you live in love, joy, peace, patience, faithfulness, kindness, goodness, self-control, and gentleness.

Take a few minutes and invite the Holy Spirit to guide your day. Pray that you would be aware of what happens around you. Perhaps there will be a friend that needs encouragement or prayer. The incredible thing to know is that when you trust that the Holy Spirit inside you, you can approach these special moments empowered. So get ready!

SONGS FOR ABIDING:
"Never Alone" (Hillsong Young & Free); "Spirit of the Living God" (Vertical Church Band); "Tis So Sweet" (Jadon Lavik)

IF SOMETHING BAD HAPPENS TO MY FAMILY, I WILL BE OK BECAUSE

God promised to be with me always and to protect me.
He will help me when it gets tough.

HANNA
North Africa
Age 12

*"As I push doubt out the door,
I invite God in to work and move."*

DAY 7

All Is Not Lost

Deuteronomy 31; Psalm 14; Matthew 17; Ephesians 6

I read Exodus, Leviticus, Numbers, and Deuteronomy, and I read a lot of rules, some of which don't even make any sense to me. But I learned that these chapters of rules are about the message God was sending to the Israelites: He was coming to live with them. He chose them as His people, and He ruled all aspects of their lives, from their clothes to their food. There was no separation between God and daily life; life encompassed and reflected Him. Their clothes, woven from one piece of fabric, designated them as God's chosen people. He meant for His presence to hold first place in their lives, leaving no room for idols. His all-encompassing presence was to be their identity as His people.

The same is true for me. My identity comes from God's presence in my life. God in me sets me apart from the rest of the world. God's presence in me makes me who I am. Jesus changed me forever. The Holy Spirit marks me. God is in me. But just having that information isn't enough. I want to be more and more aware of His presence. I want to become more aware of God—not just by speaking to Him, but by listening to Him and feeling Him close. I want to listen to more of what He says. I want to hang around and linger in His presence. I would love to really see His glory.

God, I make that my prayer right now, that Your presence would be super tangible around me. Is it weird to ask You to be dripping off me, like I've been absolutely soaked in a rainstorm? That will surely cause people to wonder what is different about me.

Why do I want this so bad? Because I know that God's presence changes everything, and everything in Libya could use His change. So I ask Him for His presence every day, for Him to come, for Him to move, because I see that without His presence I am dry, my plans fail, my ideas fall apart, and I bear (have) no fruit. I seek and desire God because I need His presence is my life. His presence is the victory, and living here among the lost of Libya, it's easy to feel surrounded and in need of a victory. Psalm 14 talks about those who say there is no god and who devour people like eating bread (vv. 1, 4). The psalmist writes that evil is in all of humanity: "There is none who does good, no, not one" (v. 3). But verse five gives a different picture about the enemy's camp: "There they are in great fear, for God is with the generation of the righteous." And that is how I feel sometimes here, surrounded by the enemy who says Jesus is not God.

When I read that verse a while ago, I remembered a scene from the movie "The Lord of the Rings: The Return of the King." It's the last charge where Gandalf, Aragorn, Legolas, and Gimli, and the small army with them—a little speck of good—are surrounded by so much evil—the armies of Mordor. The enemy's camp is around the "righteous." Gandalf and company have been fighting for a long time, but they decide to make one last charge to give Frodo and Sam one last chance to reach Mount Doom to destroy the ring. Their army was way outnumbered, but standing at the gates of Mordor, a little light shined. All was not lost, and hope remained for two hobbits on the mountain.

"For God is with the generation of the righteous." Nothing seems hopeless in God's presence. I might feel like I am somewhere far away on a mountain called Doom, deep inside Mordor, but hope is not lost for Someone walks with me. His presence abides in me. The battle is not lost at the fiery mountain, or at the dark gates, or in the desert of Libya, for the Lord walks before, and the victory is coming if I will fight on in the presence of God. God's presence is the victory, and as I wait on Him, He will fight for me.

Abide in Him

We are complete when our identities rest in Jesus alone. Are you confident that your identity rests in Jesus alone? Write your thoughts down.

When you are weak, struggling, or tired, how do you handle it? Take some notes on it.

Do you long to experience the presence of Jesus all day—beyond just your devotional time? How so?

Your victories and battles do not determine your walk with the Lord. You do not have to be far from God when things get difficult. You either can fight on, in the presence of God, or you can feel alone. Ask the Lord to give you a deeper desire for His presence so when difficult times come you know how to handle it. God's presence is the victory. Talk to the Lord for a few minutes and share where you are currently. The great news is it's never too late. You can choose to seek His presence today—in this moment, until you go to sleep tonight.

SONGS FOR ABIDING:
"Spirit Move" (Kalley Heiligenthal); "Unstoppable God" (Elevation Worship); "Holy Spirit" (Byran & Katie Torwalt)

SOMETHING THAT SCARES ME IS

I'm scared that I could live knowing the truth and happiness and not share it, to get to heaven and look down at hell and see one friend look up at me and realize, "It's my fault you're there, and not up here with me." I dread getting to heaven and not seeing people that I knew there with me. That's what scares me. A life lived for myself, a wasted and meaningless life.

LUKE
Egypt
Age 18

"*My identity comes from God's presence in my life.*"

DAY
8

There's Always More to Learn

Joshua 1; Psalm 119; Mark 8; Colossians 3

Missionary kid life comes with many challenges. One of my biggest challenges is language. Language requires a lot of time, effort and practice, and for me, a lot of tears. I am a pretty impatient learner, I admit. I don't want to spend hours studying—I want to learn it now. But even through my impatience and my tears, I know learning the local language is super important because it gives me the chance to effectively share the gospel in the language these people best understand. It also connects me to them because they are so touched by the effort. Sometimes when I try to speak Arabic, they smile and exclaim, "You're Libyan!" I love that they at least smile, even if they don't understand a word that I said.

Learning can be fun, and it can be exhausting and hard, but I think it's always rewarding. And the reward isn't just a good grade (though I do like getting those). For me, the reward of language learning is the smile on a woman's face when she hears my humbling and stumbling attempts at Arabic. The reward is the knowledge I gained that I can use for the work of Jesus. Learning builds me up (though sometimes, it tears me down first) so I can better serve Jesus and others. I don't learn something for the sake of being smart. This isn't just about something that happens in my head. I'm learning something that connects with my heart. I make the decision to take in information that will serve the world around me.

Being a learner is not something I do just for school. It's not like once I'm done with high school or university or grad school then I'm done with learning. Learning is actually something I need to incorporate into my life. It's a lifestyle, and it's lifelong. I learn so I can grow—whether that is growing in my relationship with Jesus or growing in my Arabic. This is definitely not something that happens in a moment (much like character!).

I've already discovered there can be a cycle to learning if I'm not careful. For instance, sometimes I feel too proud to say I don't know or too proud to admit I'm wrong because I've got a reputation to keep. So maybe I get a little defensive and try to prove myself right, whether or not I know what I'm talking about, and then the truth comes out—and I'm wrong! Now I'm embarrassed, or even worse humiliated. My pride takes a hit. Rather than remembering the lessons of grace or humility or love for another person, I once again try to grab it all for myself. How glad I am for Jesus, the most patient teacher. He never gives up on me—the disciple who is always messing up, complaining, arguing about who the greatest is, or misunderstanding what He's saying. I am learning always, still.

Rabbis in Jesus' day had groups of disciples. The rabbis were not like Sunday school teachers or small group leaders—volunteers that led a dozen students in Bible study. No, the rabbis were the masters. If I were a disciple of a rabbi, he would be my only teacher. Disciples lived their lives with their rabbi, and their greatest hope was to be like their famous rabbi someday. They were who their rabbi was. Their master defined them. The disciples of Jesus followed Him, watched and learned from everything He did—and in the end they were transformed into His likeness. Now I'm not first pick material—and really no one is—but Jesus still invites me to follow Him and become His disciple, to follow Him as my Teacher and learn. Living every day with Jesus transforms me into His image.

What am I learning while living in Libya? I am learning the daily challenge of speaking a new language. I am learning to go with the flow and that it's okay that I don't always know what I'm doing or where I am exactly. I am learning to depend on Jesus and on others. I'm learning to never give up, no matter the circumstances.

Learning can be both easy and tough. Learning moves me outside my comfort zones and gives me the chance to admit what I don't know and what I need to learn (or re-learn). Learning happens one step at a time, one day at a time. Learning happens as I experience life, as I make choices and as I choose to learn from them. Learning happens as I take God's Word and apply it to the moments of life. Learning can be a sacrifice but it's a sacrifice worth making.

Abide in Him

This is not about being a good student or poor student. Learning is about collecting knowledge and information that will help you interact with the world around you. Do you like to learn? We're encouraged to learn one new thing a day. Make a space in your journal for this. Write down one new thing you learn each day.

Growth can hurt sometimes, and lifelong learning requires an openness to being taught even when it hurts. Do you have a desire to grow even when it hurts? Write down your thoughts.

What is your biggest challenge right now? What has it been teaching you?

Has there ever been something in your life that you thought you learned, but then you found yourself re-learning it all over again? Take a few minutes to journal about the lessons learned.

SONGS FOR ABIDING:
"Here's My Heart" (Lauren Daigle); "Ask" (BJ Putnam ft. Jonathan Stockstill); "Be Thou My Vision" (Ascend the Hill)

WHEN I AM SCARED, JESUS HELPS ME BY

Overcoming fear.

DAVID & SARA
North Africa
Ages 10 & 9

"Learning happens as I experience life, as I make choices and as I choose to learn from them."

DAY 9

Be Grateful for Your Free Refills

Daniel 1; Psalm 28; John 14; Acts 12

I'm so glad I'm a missionary kid. I think it's awesome. Sure, there are a lot of changes in life that can be hard. It's hard to say goodbye to people and places. It's scary to go somewhere new. But I love living overseas, even though I miss some things in America like free refills on sodas and nice green grass.

My family always tries to prepare ourselves when we move, but we've learned we just can't be prepared for everything. We lived in another country in East Africa before we lived in Libya. We lived there for five years and were really happy. We thought we'd be there forever—until our whole team was kicked out. At the time we were actually outside the country, so we couldn't even go back to get our stuff. We lost all the belongings we stored there. There were no goodbyes to the people or the city that we'd never see again. I said goodbye to my best friend when we left for furlough from the first country—not knowing I wouldn't get to return and see her. That was hard. While God called us to that country, we know that He ultimately called us to unreached people, so we moved to another country in the Middle East and studied Arabic for two years until we moved here.

Every country I've lived in has been different with things I loved about each and things I found challenging about each. In one country people invited us off the street for tea, whereas in another country it took a lot more effort to build relationships. We went from being on a team of 60 people to here just being a team of us—my family. We moved from a developing, third world country to one where the people by comparison are rich. We've moved from Africa to the America, which is a major culture shock (and where I still get excited over water fountains because they're free!). We moved from the desert where we had little concept of grass to a place where no one in the family could stop reaching down and petting all the green grass we saw. When I was in America, there wasn't anyone yelling, "Foreigner!" No one stared at me as I walked by, and no one asked for a photo with us. No little children with big smiles peeked from behind the doors.

Change can hurt, but I don't resent it. I loved life in each of these unique places. I have no regrets. All the changes have shaped me, and I've learned to embrace the change that comes with being a missionary kid. I can love life here today, but be willing to leave tomorrow if that's God's plan. I know I've lost some things—material possessions, best friends, and some amount of certainty—but I've also gained more—a family in Christ that I love, all the places I've visited and people I've met. So if they kick us from this country, too, I want to hold loosely to it all. I will fully enjoy life today but be ready for what God has tomorrow.

One thing I realized is that I can't base my happiness or my identity on living in a particular city or having access to a best friend or enjoying the availability of free refills. When I attach my happiness or my identity to any one fixed thing, I know I'll become very disappointed and hurt when I'm forced to leave that one thing behind. Things, places, and people are not enough. I shouldn't cling to those things. I should only cling to the One who moves with me—Jesus. If I cling to things, it'll be harder to move, but if I cling to Jesus, the change will be less difficult. So I am learning to let go and be ready for life today with Jesus.

I do love being a missionary kid. How many teenagers like me get to watch her younger siblings play airport security like it's totally normal? How many walk past mud huts in Kenya with squawking chickens and giggling children then take a late night flight and find themselves in loud and crazy Cairo, Egypt the next day? It is pretty awesome, and I can't imagine life any other way. Accepting this as the life God has for me means I don't miss out on anything. He provides exactly what I need at the right place and the right time. I need only to cling to Jesus.

Abide in Him

How many times have you moved? What big changes have you experienced in life? How did you handle them?

What changes are in your near future? How are you planning for them? Can you?

One thing Joy realized is that she can't attach her happiness or identity to a place, person, or thing. What is your identity tied to?

Is there something in your life that you shouldn't be clinging to at the moment? Take that something and hand it to God right now. Ask Him to take its place in your life.

Clinging by definition means "overly dependent to someone or something emotionally." If you were to lose everything today, would you be truly content just having Jesus? Take a couple minutes and talk with Jesus about this. Pray He would become the only One you would cling to and that He would remove anything that can take His place.

SONGS FOR ABIDING:
"Where You Are" (Leeland); "Fierce" (Jesus Culture); "Oceans (Where Feet May Fail)" (Hillsong United)

I WOULD WANT KIDS COMING TO THE MISSION FIELD TO KNOW

That yes, it's hard to live away from your family and everything you're used to, but if God has called you to the mission field, He has something special in mind for you.

ELLA GRACE
North Africa
Age 12

LIVE DEAD LIFE

"I need only to cling to Jesus."

DAY 10

More Than Once

Genesis 12; Psalm 128; Luke 11; Romans 3

I went bungee jumping once. I freaked out completely—before I even did the jumping part! I am not a super talkative person, but that day I was. Fear paralyzed my body, but my mouth chattered away in my nervousness. I just kept talking. I couldn't stop! I can't explain it, and it hasn't happened since. So strange, but so funny—ask anyone who was there.

How often have I viewed my decision to follow Jesus that way—like it was a one-time-can't-explain-it experience? I raised my hand and accepted Jesus as Savior, and life was never the same. It only happened once, and such a moment hasn't happened since. But what I've discovered is that this decision to follow Jesus, my surrender to Him, was not a one-time deal, but a daily deal. When I accepted Jesus as Savior and started to follow Him, the road to heaven didn't end there—it started there.

Surrender is a place where Jesus is the road and the destination and the travel partner. He is everything to me as I move forward in surrender. I don't walk halfway down the road and turn back. I move forward in Him, through Him, and with Him. So unlike my bungee jump experience, which was down and back again, my surrender to Jesus is a daily journey of walking with Him, learning from Him, and trusting Him. I see each new day as a chance to take a step of faith on the road with Jesus. It is the choice of trust I make—to let go of my obsessive desire for control. Jesus, please, take the wheel! Give me what I need, not what I want. This daily surrender gives me peace and purpose.

As God gives me life, He doesn't give it so I can keep it for myself. God gives it so I can give it back. This is my chance to express the love that He shows to me, back to Him. I have one life to spend, and one death to give, so what happens when I stop trying to steal the gift He has given and instead offer it back? What happens when I let go of my plan and follow His, no matter how inconvenient? Choosing to live dead points me in that direction, to constantly turn things over to Jesus. I pray for His will to be done in me and with me, no matter the cost, even if the cost is my life.

So I choose obedience. Obedience says "no" to the wrong things and "yes" to the God things (including the people He places over me). Though it sounds clear-cut, it doesn't make this obedience thing any easier. I have to remember that my feelings don't always come first. When I make a commitment, I commit to doing something no matter what, even though some days I just don't feel like it. I want to give Jesus my best, which might take some extra effort of denying myself for a "yes" to Jesus. Obedience is a choice, a choice to live out the commitments I make daily. There's a hymn that says, "Trust and obey for there is no other way to be happy in Jesus but to trust and obey." Obedience is not about being good, but about doing something out of love and reverence for Jesus. I need to obey Jesus (and those He places over me) as an act of love.

I am learning that God will continue to ask me to take another step, to go deeper, to give Him another "yes." This daily dying, this daily surrender is the path to follow. I want my life to continually be given to God. So when I feel myself saying "no," I need to remind myself that I am not in a bungee jump moment—I am not down and back again. Instead, I am walking down the road and going the extra mile with Jesus. There is so much down this road I cannot yet see, so I will put on that armor of God and follow Him to live a life without borders—to learn from Him, to obey Him, to trust Him, to surrender to Him, and to say "yes" to Him.

Abide in Him

Think back to the moment you accepted Jesus as your Savior. What was that moment like? What things did you have to obediently need to say "no" to after accepting Jesus as your Savior? Praise God for those victories!

Take a few minutes to search your heart. Ask yourself these questions and once you feel like you're released from your asking, write down your answers:

1. What is the purpose in being obedient to Jesus?
2. Do you enjoy saying "yes" to Him, or do you find it difficult to be fully committed?
3. How does you daily obedience look like today?
4. Do you have a burning desire to learn, obey, trust, and be completely surrendered, regardless of how you might feel?

It's always important to see where your heart is currently. When we long to glorify Jesus in all that we do, our daily obedience becomes easier. It will not always be easy, but know that you are never alone in the process! Praise God at where you are today and the person you are becoming.

SONGS FOR ABIDING:
"To Worship You I Live" (Israel & the New Breed); "Faithful to the End" (Paul McClure, Hannah McClure, Bethel Music); "Trust and Obey" (Big Daddy Weave)

I THINK FACING SAD AND BAD THINGS ON THE FIELD IS WORTH IT BECAUSE

We know that everything we do or everything that happens to us is a part of God's plan.

E. F.
North Africa
Age 15

"I am learning that God will continue to ask me to take another step, to go deeper, to give Him another 'yes.'"

Abide

ABIDING
CHARACTER
SPIRIT EMPOWERMENT
LIFELONG LEARNING

With time and some life experience, my understanding of these values has grown. Below are my thoughts now on what these values mean. Take a few minutes to reflect on the definitions you wrote earlier and consider if you might improve on them.

ABIDING:

Christianity is not just a religion. Following Jesus is a relationship. My view of abiding expanded from a few quick minutes to the phrase: "Talk the walk, walk the talk." Abiding became my relationship to God and how I walked with Jesus throughout my day.

The metaphor that has most helped me understand abiding is probably one you've heard before. In John 15, Jesus declares himself the Vine and us the branches. Abiding is not how much time I spend reading in the morning, but how I connect to the Vine throughout the day. My life and my strength flow from Jesus the Vine.

I define abiding as:

CHARACTER:

I've started to see character as both what you're made of and what you do daily. Character is about the daily choice to do the right thing even when it's hard. Character is not just something that we naturally have—it's what we choose to use in our lives and thoughts and what Jesus builds in our hearts. You recognize a tree by its fruit, so what am I growing in my life today? I reap what I sow.

I define character as:

SPIRIT EMPOWERMENT:

Finding what Spirit empowerment means for me was harder than I thought. I've imagined Spirit empowerment as a powerful thunderstorm, but as I imagined that, I knew that wasn't the reality in me. Looking at my quiet self, it is different. Spirit empowerment is a powerful voice, but I realize now is that it also comes through a whisper.

When the Spirit uses us, sometimes it's just through a word—a word of encouragement, a bold question, a sacrifice of praise, or a touch of love. It can be uncomfortable. It can be hard. But it's always freeing to allow the Holy Spirit to work in and move through me in ways I never thought possible.

I define Spirit empowerment as:

LIFELONG LEARNING:

I see learning as a lifestyle, from learning language to learning love for all the people I live among. It's important to have a good attitude and to give learning my best, as unto Jesus.

I know I'm not supposed to admit this until I'm not done with school, but I really appreciate the process of learning. No, I don't always like school; it's not always easy. But with learning there's growth. The saying "You're never too old to learn something new" gets old. Learning can be tiring, and it takes humility, but it's a way of following Jesus and finding out more about Him. What learning gives is much more than it takes from you.

I define lifelong learning as:

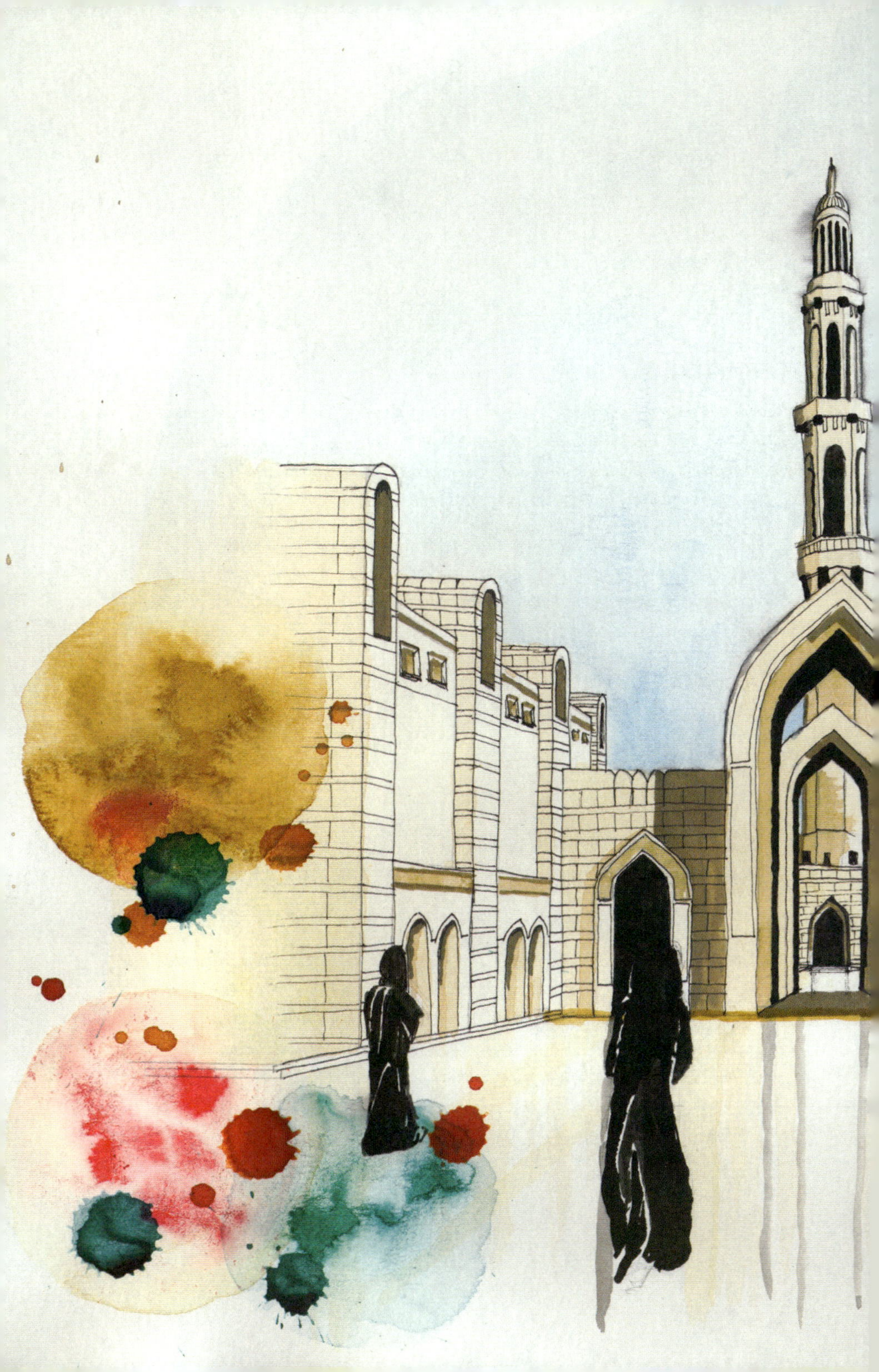

تبشير

Apostle

APOSTOLIC FUNCTION
TEAM
PARTNERSHIP
PIONEERING

This second section includes my journal entries on our core value of Apostle. Apostle means to proclaim the gospel. It took a few years and a lot of experiences to better understand how these values work in daily life. Below are my thoughts on what I thought these words meant. Take a few minutes to write your own definitions.

APOSTOLIC FUNCTION:

I guessed that it meant following the example of the apostles, like Paul visiting all those churches he planted or Peter preaching to a crowd and 3,000 people being saved in one day. Beyond that, I didn't know what it meant, but I knew it meant really big things.

I define apostolic function as:

PIONEERING:

This meant going to the unreached, where there is no gospel witness.

I define pioneering as:

TEAM:

I'm competitive, so when I think of the word "team," I think of games and who the winner will be. The problem for me is that I prefer to do things on my own, so the idea of working on a team is not really my thing.

I define team as:

PARTNERSHIP:

In context, I understood that the core value of partnership is between the local church and foreign believers because I've lived with local believers in the daily for a while now.

I define partnership as:

DAY 11

You're Invited

Nehemiah 2; Psalm 19; Matthew 10; 1 Timothy 4

Jesus is too good to keep to myself. He's worth telling the whole world. He's worth sharing with my unreached neighbors. As I abide in Jesus, I see beyond myself and through God's eyes, and I can see what He's doing in the world today.

I'll be honest. When I first heard the phrase "apostolic function," I had no idea what that meant. I just guessed that it meant following the example of the apostles—Paul planting churches around Asia and then visiting them and writing to them or Peter preaching to huge crowds and seeing 3,000 people saved in one day. I thought, "Go big or go home." I figured it was maybe even Billy Graham big and reaching all over the world.

But then I realized that apostolic function is a big deal made small. God invites me to join Him in what He is doing today. My purpose is to make God's glory known in my life and in the world among the unreached. How do I reach every tribe, every language, and every nation? I can't do it on my own. God asks me to join other Christians in apostolic function—no matter who they are or where they live. Sharing the gospel with the world takes me working together with other Christians to live and function as the body of Christ and to proclaim Jesus where the church does not exist.

I know that some will stay in their home countries while others will go, and the ones who go need the others to stay because there are plenty of things to do in the work of God's Kingdom—intercessory prayer, financial support, and mobilization. I make the choice to get on board (with my family) for those who have never heard. I know that while not everyone will go, everyone should ask the question, "Am I willing to go if God asks?" And if they don't go, they ask, "What does one do if one does not go?"

We each have a part to play, but no matter the role, we all have the same focus. Whether we go or support or inspire others to go, it all works toward the same destination—planting the church where it doesn't exist. We need each other—we cannot do the work alone. The one person on the field needs another person praying for her, praying for the people she's reaching. I need teenagers who are not missionary kids praying for me and my siblings and my parents. The church globally stands with the workers on the field.

Teenagers, like me, are part of apostolic function. The question is not if God is asking us to do something—because He is. The question is, "What?" I ask God what He is calling me to do and then I do my best to follow that call. Sometimes I miss what God asks me to do or I ignore or debate His words (like Jonah in some ways). Often as I process what I'm hearing, I talk to my mom or my dad or maybe another team member. If I was in America, I would probably also talk to my youth pastor. If the path isn't exactly clear, I just keep asking Him and trust that He'll make it clear in time.

Because I do believe that God has a specific purpose for each of His children, I know I have a role in His Kingdom work. It just takes the decision to step out into God's world and do my part. Right now, it's taking the opportunities He brings to tell a Libyan girl about Jesus. Right now, it's about crying in prayer for broken and hurting people. Right now, it's about advocating for the unreached and mobilizing others to go. (That's why I'm writing this journal!)

I'm not sure where I'll end up in the future, but I know I'll be part of this "apostolic function." I accepted God's invitation to the work. This is God's work, but He invites me and other believers as His body, the body of Christ, to the work. He calls us to be workers on the field; He calls us to be advocates in prayer; He calls us to be mobilizers, sharing our passion for God's global mission; and He calls us to be givers, supporting the work. I might not know exactly where I'll be after I graduate, but I know that I won't be alone because apostolic function requires all of us for the work of reaching the unreached.

YOU'RE INVITED

Abide in Him

Joy wrote: "But then I realized that apostolic function is a big deal made small. God invites me to join Him in what He is doing today." Do you believe that God has chosen you to be a part of what He is doing all around you? Write down your thoughts.

Take a moment and think about where God has placed you today. Think about the kind of people you are surrounded by or the ones you interact with every day. Imagine what it would be like if everyone around you was talking about Jesus. Imagine conversations that included "Jesus changed my life!"

Ask God what your role is supposed to be to see those images come true. Write what comes to your heart.

Now take a moment and think about the nations, missionaries, and their families. God calls you to be a part of what He is doing in the world—not only where He has you, but globally. Isn't that exciting? Take few minutes and ask God to reveal how you will partner globally in apostolic function. Perhaps it's giving, praying, or even going. Whichever it is, your role is very important. Believe that you are a part of something greater than you. Make some notes of your thoughts now.

SONGS FOR ABIDING:
"Nearness" (Jenn Johnson, Bethel); "Let There Be Light" (Bryan & Katie Torwalt); "So Will I (100 Billion X)" (Hillsong United)

I LOVE BEING A MISSIONARY KID BECAUSE

Being a missionary kid is cool because we get to see firsthand what God is doing and we get to be a part of it. We get to witness to people and share the gospel with them. It's really awesome.

J. E.
North Africa
Age 17

LIVE DEAD LIFE

"Jesus is too good to keep to myself."

DAY 12

His Heartbeat

Jeremiah 17; Psalm 73; Matthew 9; 2 Corinthians 5

The news can easily discourage me with so much talk of death, war, and disease. I just want to look away and pretend I didn't hear or see any of it. It would be so much easier to just live in my own little world, all by myself.

The problem with this hermit outlook is Jesus. When Jesus saw the need, He had compassion. He saw sheep without a shepherd. He saw the lost and blind. He didn't turn His face away, and He never pretended they didn't exist. Jesus came to earth, lived among the lost, and loved them. He loved them and loved me enough to die for all of us.

Honestly, there is nothing special about me that drives me to want to reach the unreached and to serve others. I don't love that much. I'm not that generous. I can be selfish. I don't care enough about others to do much of anything for them. But God does. God doesn't ask me to find the love inside me for these people. No, God invites me to share His love because that's where love begins and ends—with Him. My love will eventually fail. But God's love will not.

The way that I found God's heart for unreached people groups is by drawing closer to Him. I can't grow closer to God without feeling what He feels in return—His passion, love, pain, joy, mission, and heart. God's heartbeat becomes my heartbeat. The desire to plant the church where it does not exist is God's heart beating in me. My willingness to speak the gospel and to be His hands and feet is a gift that God delights in. He delights to give me His heart, and His heart compels me to action. For this to happen, I need to be soft to God's touch and open to His voice and His plans. I have to be open and willing—not building walls or drawing lines, limiting God or myself. When I am open to God and His love, I can stand with my sisters around the world and be near them with my prayers. I can go and work among them and, if necessary, suffer with them.

This is the cry of apostolic function—it's my longing joined with God's longing that all would hear the gospel. I invite God to shape my heart into someone He can use, to give me His eyes for the unreached to see beyond, and to make my heart more like His. He then invites me into His work to take part in apostolic function, to see His glory among all nations. This cry of apostolic function gives me the heart of an advocate, gives me the passion to mobilize, gives me the vision to pray, and gives me the openness to go. I will pour out my life, my time, my money, my life, and my heart, and I will encourage others to do the same. Then I, plus my family, plus our team, plus our supporters, plus the praying strangers become the body of Christ, planting the church together.

In Matthew 9:35–38, Jesus and His disciples do two things: they pray for the harvest and for laborers. Then in chapter 10, Jesus sends the disciples out. The disciples dared to pray and then Jesus sent them out as the answer to their prayer. It is through the cry of a broken, lost world that I hear Jesus call me. Do I dare to pray for the harvest and for workers? Do I dare to be the answer to the prayer?

When I cry out to Jesus, God delights to give an answer, and the answer is Himself—His heart in us. Then when I cry out for more, the answer is again Himself! When I cry for a broken world, hurt people, evil things, a deep wound, or gaping holes in hearts, God delights to be the answer to my prayers. He is the answer. I was never meant to be the answer to a lost, broken world. I am just meant to be in the place God calls me to be, to be able to tell the lost that He hears, that He hasn't forgotten, that He knows. To do that, I have to live near them and I have to keep them always in my prayers.

Abide in Him

Joy said, "God doesn't ask me to find the love inside me for these people. No, God invites me to share His love because that's where love begins and ends—with Him. My love will eventually fail. But God's love will not." On our own it is practically impossible to love and have a heart for the lost, so instead we draw nearer to God so His love flows through us. Have you experienced that?

Finding God's heart for unreached people groups happens by drawing closer to Him. As you do, you will feel more of what He feels. Joy wrote, "His passion, love, pain, joy, mission, and heart. God's heartbeat becomes my heartbeat. The desire to plant the church where it does not exist is God's heart beating in me." Are you open and willing to allow God to give you the desires of His heart?

Have you limited Jesus or built walls out of fear? Take a few minutes and draw closer to Jesus right now. Pray that every day Jesus would increase your desire to draw closer to Him, and as you do, you will find God's heart for the unreached. Your willingness and desires will become more kingdom minded.

SONGS FOR ABIDING:
"Heartbeat" (Mosaic MSC); "I Can't Believe" (Elevation Worship); "This We Know" (Passion, Kristian Stanfill)

LIVING IN MY COUNTRY IS DIFFICULT BECAUSE

It's hard to get things I want, like my favorite candy, and sometimes it can be hard to communicate with boys my age because of the language.

BENJAMIN
North Africa
Age 10

"The way that I found God's heart for unreached people groups is by drawing closer to Him."

DAY 13

Somebody's Watching Me
1 Samuel 16; Psalm 29; Matthew 5; James 1

Ever get the feeling you're being watched? I do, every day. Seriously, an American family living in Libya is the complete opposite of a "Where's Waldo?" book. There's no hiding here. It's pretty obvious we're not from around these parts. (Though I've been tempted to put a red-and-white-striped hat and shirt on my little brother just for kicks.)

We know that people always have an eye on what we're doing. While we don't want to fake it and act like everything is wonderful all the time, we do want our lives to be a testimony to them. They see how we treat each other. This can be challenge but it's also an opportunity. Being on display as the body of Christ in this country is a chance for Jesus to shine from us and for us to live the message we proclaim, so that these lovely Libyans will see the love of Christ.

Since I've grown up as a missionary kid, it can be easy to forget that we're here as ambassadors of Jesus. This fact should change how I act. It should change me. All that I do should be living life for the glory of God. First Corinthians 10:31 says, "Therefore, whether you eat or drink, or whatever you do, do all to the glory of God." How do we do all for the glory of God? Well, "for the glory of God" means that the purpose ends with God, not with me. What I do is not about me, but about God. Reading my Bible isn't about me, but Jesus. Visiting my neighbor isn't about me, but Jesus. Serving tea isn't about me, but Jesus. Washing the dishes, exercising, and worshiping are not about me, but Jesus. Jesus takes the spotlight, and His story takes center stage. As an ambassador I represent Someone from another kingdom—Jesus. So in everything I do, is it Jesus they see?

People will see Jesus by the way I live, but sometimes I feel like a blurred image of Him, like I am in no way a clear image of Christ. On those days the only way for others to see Him is for me to get out of the way, to surrender to Him and let Him clean away the smudges. God could choose to do His work differently. He could send angels in a blaze of glory from heaven to my Libyan neighbors. But He doesn't—He sends me.

There is a responsibility in knowing and loving Jesus. Does my life bear fruit for His glory? I have the responsibility to share Jesus in every way I can. Giving glory to God through my mouth and my actions isn't always easy, but thank God, He gives me grace—so much grace. He gives me what I will never deserve to change me into what I could never become by myself. God gives me the grace to live dead. He gives me the grace to do what I never dared, to go where I never thought I could, and to be someone I never imagined.

I do "all for the glory of God" by living my life fully in His presence. I do "all for the glory of God" by listening to His voice and being obedient. I do "all for the glory of God by making every task an act of worship. I chose to live purposefully, to share the meaning of Jesus, and to not waste anything God gives me.

The glory of God is my purpose. It's why I'm here on this earth until the day Jesus takes me home. Therefore, I aim to make Jesus known in all I say and do. I live for the glory of God to be displayed in me, and I desire to proclaim what Jesus has done for me and for others.

Abide in Him

Who you represent yourself to be is vital to your Christian walk. As a Christian, do you feel like your being watched? What do others say about you?

Do you feel like you represent Jesus well in the way you interact with those around you?

Do you view the way you act and the reason that you do things as glorifying to Jesus?

There is a responsibility in knowing and loving Jesus. Does your life bear fruit for His glory?

When you do all things for the glory of God, you will have a deeper urgency to want to represent Jesus well. Take a few minutes and search your heart. Ask God to reveal areas you need to give to Him. Perhaps it's the way you interact or represent yourself. Maybe you aren't living in a way that strives to bring God glory. If that's the case, know that it's okay, and it can change right now. Give Jesus the best of your time and receive His grace.

SONGS FOR ABIDING:
"Our Father" (Bethel); "Oh Lord, You're Beautiful" (Jesus Culture); "Isn't the Name" (Covenant Worship)

ONE THING JESUS HAS TAUGHT ME ABOUT MISSIONS IS

The work isn't as glorious and rewarding as one might think. Even after investing years of effort and prayer, the harvest might only involve one or two new Christians—and not a church or rock solid believers, but a couple worried and scared converts.

ZACK
Egypt
Age 17

"I do 'all for the glory of God' by living my life fully in His presence."

DAY 14

Scouring the Land
Numbers 13; Psalm 51; John 1; Romans 10

"What are you doing here?" These are most often the first words people say to my family when they meet us. They're always amazed that we live here. It truly means something to them that we chose to be here with them when we could literally be anywhere else in the world. To them, Libya is the last place an American would chose to live.

As I thought about the Libyans' consistent and amazed response to my family living here, Jesus came to mind. Jesus crossed an even larger gap when He came to earth as a baby. How amazing is it that Jesus left heaven for earth and dwelt among us to die for our sins! That's the much better story—more important than my family's move! When I stop and think about that, my mind nearly explodes. If Jesus would go that far for me, I can certainly go to the ends of the earth for Him.

The word "pioneer" is often used to describe a foot soldier that prepared the way for the army. A pioneer was a scout. Pioneer missionaries go to the places where the church of Jesus does not exist, to places where Jesus is not worshiped. These pioneers declare Jesus in the most open way possible and in the closest way possible because Jesus does not offer His gift of salvation from far away. He comes close and heals and saves in the middle of the war, poverty, pain, famine, and even wealth. No matter how far He must go, no matter how hard the land, no matter how insecure it sounds, Jesus goes because that is what He does. We go because Jesus goes.

Pioneer missionaries, like those on my team, are people who prepare the way for others to follow. Others will build on what all of us do now. In the days and years to come, there will be leaders like Caleb who have a vision for the land and there will be people who will pray and claim God's promise for the land. Not everyone will be a pioneer missionary, but everyone needs a vision to see beyond the borders of her country and have the courage to send others, and the pioneers are the ones who scout the land and report back home to those future missionaries and intercessors.

To pioneer is to obey and walk by faith, not sight. To pioneer is to face frustration and sow the seeds of gospel in obedience. I cannot not go because the risk is too great. I cannot not follow Jesus because I'm afraid of the cost. Yes, there will be risks if all people are to hear the gospel. There will be danger. I will feel lonely. My pride will be damaged. When all of that happens, I must determine once again that Jesus is worth it.

This life sounds adventurous and exciting, maybe even a little glamorous, and while life might have moments of adventure and excitement, I have yet to see much glamour. Pioneering—scouting the land—is not easy; it's often hard and lonely. In those moments, I must be aware of whispers in my ear—the lies that the enemy tries to sell me. If I'm not mindful, I can get stuck believing the lies, which bring discouragement and grumblings and a quitter's attitude. This is why abiding is so important! Thankfully, I can call on Jesus and He draws close. He is here on the frontier with me. I am never alone and never forgotten, and He is worth any inconvenience, any trial, any height or any depth because His love spans it all.

No matter where I go on the planet, Jesus still went farther when He came to us. If Jesus loves the people of the world that much, so must I. Love came in a way that no one else could. Love opened His arms wide to be nailed to a cross. Love died. Love defeated sin and death. Love rose again. Love made a way. If I know the cure, if I know the truth, if I know life, if I know the love—and I do—then I am compelled to share it with everyone everywhere—wherever Jesus is not yet worshipped. I am a pioneer!

Abide in Him

She mentioned that pioneers are soldiers that go and prepare the way for an army. In what ways can you be the "pioneer" wherever God has you today?

Think of your school or your job. Has anyone claimed it for Jesus yet? Perhaps your school already has a Bible study after school or a Christian group. If not, would you imagine yourself as a pioneer to start one? Take a few minutes, and ask God to direct your next step on how you can pioneer.

Do you ever feel moments of loneliness, frustration, or doubt? Do the lies ever make you feel defeated or discouraged? Write out a prayer in your journal, asking God for strength. When those moments come, read the prayer out loud to Jesus, and leave it as His feet.

SONGS FOR ABIDING:
"The Voyage" (Amanda Cook); "Do It Again" (Elevation Worship); "Can't Stop Singing" (Covenant Worship)

JESUS IS WORTH LIVING FOR BECAUSE

He is the reason that we even DO live and breathe every day.

ELLA GRACE
North Africa
Age 12

LIVE DEAD LIFE

"To pioneer is to obey and walk by faith, not sight."

DAY 15

Adventure Time

Jeremiah 29; Psalm 40; Matthew 6; Philippians 3

Jesus tells some crazy stories. In one such story, a man found treasure hidden in a field and when he found it, he went and sold all he had and bought that field (Matt. 13:44). In another, Jesus said the kingdom of heaven is a like a merchant looking for fine pearls, when he found one of great value he went and sold all he had and bought it (Matt. 13:45–46).

We love adventure stories—stories filled with danger and suspense, a twist at every turn. We love a good story, in which characters risk everything, and sometimes they win and sometimes they lose. I think sometimes we often wish our own lives were like that—not all danger all the time, but with a promise that something exciting would happen every once in a while. I think we want more life in our life. The cry for more is one God delights to answer. He delights to answer with more of himself. There is more to life, more than what I see around me. He is that more.

One of my definitions for life here is "to push through." For example, I must keep eating as the sweet, smiling old lady gives me a heaping plate of food and says, "You're not eating enough." I have to push through even when I don't like the particular food piled on the plate. I push through until course number four, which could be slimly lamb or sheep's brains. I push through until I literally have no more space left in my body. I push through until they gift me the fat of the animal, which is their favorite part, and then I frantically signal, "No more, please, no more." I push through to find the more. I push through even when it's hard. I push through even if I have the chance to quit. I push through and persevere when it's hard. I find the more in Jesus. I fix my eyes on Him and push through.

When I start a race, it's exciting. I'm running fast and free. But after a while, I get tired. After a while longer, I start wondering if the race is even worth running. "Why am I even doing this?" I ask myself. "For a little medal? Is that worth the pain?" But when it comes to the race of life, I'm not running for a something. I'm running for Someone. I'm running for the more He gives. He is my prize. In the little moments, He is what makes the race of life worth living. He makes the race worth it. I will not find the prize by staying where I am. I need to run. I need to follow. Jeremiah 29:13 says, "You will seek me and find Me when you search for Me with all your heart." Who is my treasure? Who do I value more than anything? I run the race for the joy set before me. I run after Jesus.

I must remember what it is I chase. It's not a pot of gold at the end of the rainbow, but the joy of Jesus in heaven. Matthew 6:19–21 says, "Do not lay up for yourselves treasures on earth, where moth and rust destroy and where thieves break in and steal; but lay up for yourselves treasures in heaven, where neither moth nor rust destroys and where thieves do not break in and steal. For where your treasure is, there your heart will be also." The treasure of heaven is the goal. Jesus is the goal. More of Him is the prize, and I can find that now, for eternity. To do so, I make choices every day to obey Him by sharing the gospel with an Arab friend or refusing to get angry with a sibling. I do that by dying to what might be the wide road and chasing the treasure on a narrow road.

The road we're on is not well traveled, but I know Him who is the Way. It's not the field full of treasure or sea full of pearls, but Jesus never promised the work would be easy. So I keep moving forward. I keep running. I keep chasing Him, my prize. God is the goal. Jesus is the treasure, and the treasure is worth proclaiming to the whole world.

ADVENTURE TIME

Abide in Him

Do you remember a time you had to push through even when it was difficult to do so? Maybe you almost quit, but you knew you had to push through.

What are you chasing today? Is it good grades, athletic abilities, or other talents and hobbies?

Matthew 6:19–21 says, "Do not lay up for yourselves treasures on earth, where moth and rust destroy and where thieves break in and steal; but lay up for yourselves treasures in heaven, where neither moth nor rust destroys and where thieves do not break in and steal. For where your treasure is, there your heart will be also."

Take a few minutes to search your heart. Are you busy storing up treasures on earth? Write out what you are currently storing here on earth.

Read through the list out loud and ask Jesus to hold those things, as He becomes your goal. Invite Jesus to be your treasure, and ask for His help to make your main desire a willingness to proclaim Him.

SONGS FOR ABIDING:
"Chasing You" (Jenn Johnson, Bethel); "How Great" (Covenant Worship); "Moving Forward" (Israel Houghton)

JESUS IS WORTH DYING FOR BECAUSE

He forgives our sins.

DAVID & SARA
North Africa
Age 10 & 9

"Jesus is the treasure, and the treasure is worth proclaiming to the whole world."

DAY 16

A Voice: We All Have One

Esther 4; Psalm 27; Matthew 13; 2 Timothy 4

I'm pretty quiet and prefer not to speak. Problem is, I gave my life to Jesus, and my life includes my mouth.

I always look for an excuse so I don't have to speak. I want my outward actions to speak for me, but my actions are not enough. Actions without words cannot express the depth of Jesus' work in me. My pile of good actions is a bunch of filthy rags without the grace and mercy of Jesus. And I need to say that. I need to share the reason, that I am a sinner saved because of Jesus. I need to tell my Arab neighbors why I'm different. Because, seriously, are they supposed to guess the gospel of Jesus by watching me serve tea or help my mother? They might notice that I'm different, but they can easily pin me to the board with all the do-gooders of other faiths. If I don't speak, what makes me any different from all the other polite, nice people? I must use my voice. My lifestyle is not the way to Jesus because it is far from perfect. I blow up. I make mistakes. I go the wrong way. I make a poor choice. That's why I need to testify to Him. My lifestyle points to Jesus. It accompanies my words. There is never an excuse not to speak. Others will see Jesus in the way I live, but only after He is pointed out first. I need to "mouth point" them to Jesus.

Esther feared speaking out. For her, the cost of speaking out could be her life. It was an act that would change everything. While she wasn't sure what would happen, she placed her trust, even her life, in God's hands. "If I perish, I perish" (Esther 4:16). I struggle with this, too—the fear of standing up and speaking out. But I, like Esther, believe there is Someone before me and behind me, standing right beside me as I stand apart from the crowd. That's not something anyone wants to do. The crowd might laugh. But eternity hangs on this moment, and I have to speak. I have to stand for Someone. I don't want to be the one not found in Ezekiel 22:30: "So I sought for a man among them who would make a wall, and stand in the gap before Me on behalf of the land, that I should not destroy it; but I found no one." I want to be the one who stands in that gap. I don't want to be the one standing in the crowd, following the path everyone else follows, going where everyone else goes. There's nothing wrong with wanting to be liked, but to what end? I must speak, just like Esther, because people's lives are on the line. I can stand in front of my authorities, my neighbors, my peers, and my world, and share the truth of Jesus.

For some, sharing the gospel seems to come so naturally. I find it hard. I find it much easier to serve and show them Jesus in other ways, but that's still not an excuse not to share. I can't keep this hope to myself. I need to push through the discomfort even when I don't know what to say. I need to push past what feels uncomfortable for them to meet Jesus. Life here creates opportunities for the gospel pretty naturally, but sometimes I'm afraid to take them. I second-guess if it's the right moment, or I doubt my language skill. Sometimes I value sounding smart or right more than I value the opportunity. When I share something, I want them to say "wow" or "yes." I want to manipulate the truth into a way that puts me in a good light when really I just have to share the truth. The truth needs to be told because it changes everything. Their response is not my responsibility. I am not responsible for the outcome. I pray that seed lands on good soil, but I can't make it sprout. The Holy Spirit brings life. I just scatter the seeds.

In the Muslim world and in many other places, the call to prayer sounds fives times a day from the mosque. Whenever I hear it, I feel the need to lift the name of Jesus, to praise Him, to bring light into the darkness. I use my voice to speak the name of Jesus in a place where His name is not exalted. I have a voice and I will use it. I will use it to push back the darkness and share the light of Jesus. It might feel like I'm talking to a wall and nothing is getting through, but I will use the voice God has given me.

Abide in Him

It's going to take boldness to proclaim Jesus with your mouth, and it might feel uncomfortable at times. Joy said, "I need to push through the discomfort even when I don't know what to say. I need to push past what feels uncomfortable for them to meet Jesus." What are some ways you can share Jesus throughout your day today? It could be as simple as praying for someone, inviting a friend to church, or sharing why you love Jesus. Make a list.

Take a few minutes and pray for opportunities to share about Jesus. Ask God that you would be aware of those moments. Remember that God goes before you and that you are never alone!

Go a step further. Pray that you would meet people who are ready for Jesus but simply need someone to share the gospel with them. You can be that person!

SONGS FOR ABIDING:
"Behold (Then Sings My Soul)" (Hillsong Worship); "When You Walk Into the Room" (Byran & Katie Torwalt); "Ever Be" (Bethel Music)

IF SOMETHING BAD HAPPENS TO MY FAMILY, I WILL BE OKAY BECAUSE

I am not that scared for my family's safety because I believe that God will protect us. But if something terrible did happen to my family, I would know that it serves a purpose in God's plan. Nothing surprises God. If I'm ever afraid, I pray about the situation or just speak the name Jesus.

LOGAN
North Africa
Age 17

LIVE DEAD LIFE

"I want to be the one who stands in that gap."

DAY 17

Waiting for My Shoes
Ezekiel 2; Psalm 63; Luke 9; Acts 13

The sheer number of lost people around us is overwhelming. Many are hopeless and desperate as they realize the situation in their country is not getting any better. But we believe that the light of Jesus is shining brighter as each new person only adds to that light in a dark land. That's why daily life as a team begins with prayer. We meet four days a week and pray for the nation. We use a list and lift up all the names we can remember. Entering God's presence is a great way to have God's heart for the people even before we step out the door.

And I need God's heart because as a team, we make some interesting visits. One such visit I made with my mom, sister, and another female team member was with some sisters and their mother, women we met in our neighborhood. This house is not enjoyable to visit. I always have to mentally and spiritually prepare myself before I walk through the door. The mother is older and pushy, and on a previous visit, she tried to force us to say the Shahada, the phrase one recites to become a Muslim. Their idea of personal space is far different from mine with people always talking in my face, and I never quite know what strange situation we might find ourselves in, such as on this particular visit. After an hour our team decided to wrap the visit up, but the mother was having none of it. Deciding it was not time for us to leave, she hid our shoes! I wasn't too happy about staying or about my missing shoes, but what could I do? I gave a wistful glance to the street as she pulled me back into the house.

This family is not the one I would choose to spend my time with, but I realize I'm terrible at telling who the hungry ones are. Multiple opportunities to share the gospel have come through our relationship with this family—one sister eagerly received a Bible from us while another began our conversation with the question, "What is the difference between our religions?" We shared that Jesus is the only Way, Truth, and Life. The difficult circumstances in their lives and in their country are making them more open to the gospel. People outside look at the situation in Libya and say, "Why don't you wait until things calm down before you go?" I say because the time is now. I don't want to lose any opportunity as we encounter people who are more open to the gospel than ever before.

I used to think of team as a big group of people because that's what I knew. When I was younger in a different country, our team was over sixty people. Our team now, which is only a year old, is different and smaller; it's mainly comprised of my immediate family. With so few team members and so many lost people, it would be easy to believe that we can't make much of a difference, but even though we're few in number, I see where God is opening doors, even if someone hides my shoes in the process. I push through, and we press on together as a team.

In a place with so few believers, it's easy to feel isolated, so being part of a team is just a healthier way to do life here. Fellowship with other believers reminds me that I am not alone in this, that my family is not alone in this. Everyone on the team has a place and everyone carries part of the load. Our game nights, walks at the park, and trips to the beach all help me see how we are better together, how we can do more and be more for Jesus than if we all just tried it alone.

Life would be different with a larger team—in some ways easier and in other ways harder. There would be more hands and voices for the work, but there would also be more hands and voices to get along with. So I'll take our little team for now and share my life with them. I'll walk this road day in and day out with them. I'll enjoy their company around the dinner table and together we'll wait patiently for the return of our shoes.

Abide in Him

Have you considered meeting with other Christians to pray for your community leaders, schools, churches, and the lost?

Libya is not an easy place to live, and as Joy mentioned, people often question why her family decided to live and share Jesus there now instead of waiting for the country to calm down. What are your thoughts on that?

Think about where God has you now. Do you sometimes wait for your friends to be more open to Jesus? Do you sometimes avoid those that you think will never want to hear about Jesus?

Take a few minutes to pray for boldness. Pray that you would never rely on your feelings when sharing the gospel, but on the beautiful truth that Jesus is the only way. So many around you have yet to experience the freedom you have.

SONGS FOR ABIDING:
"One Thirst and Hunger" (Bethel); "All the Poor and Powerless" (All Sons & Daughters); "No One Higher" (Seth Condrey)

SOMETHING THAT SCARES ME IS

Often I'm scared that a young man we pass on the street might harass us, particularly when I'm the only brother with my sisters. When I'm scared, I go to Jesus with my worries and He gives me peace.

ABRAM
North Africa
Age 13

LIVE DEAD LIFE

"In a place with so few believers, it's easy to feel isolated..."

DAY 18

My Strengthening Love

Isaiah 41; Psalm 3; Mark 4; Ephesians 2

Many people here are afraid, and every time we leave the country, they ask if we're coming back. "Yes, of course," we answer. It makes no sense to them that we choose to live here at a time when the country is unstable and when all they want to do is leave. My mom and I recently met two ladies at a café. They were so amazed that we decided to live here, so my mom explained how Jesus gives us the peace to live here. One lady asked, "Can we video you saying that? Because if I tell my friends that an American lady is living here, and she's not afraid, they would never believe it." My mom agreed and the lady took the video of my mom sharing the peace of Christ. Watch for us on YouTube.

I believe God called my family here. Some say it's unwise and foolish to risk living here, but I have peace, and my family has peace. Though I will admit that with everything happening here, being at peace isn't always easy. Still I know that I stand on a Rock that can never be shaken because my peace is not based on circumstances, people, or places, but on Jesus. What's awesome is that peace is available to everyone—to everyone in Libya and to everyone reading this. Jesus never changes. He is the Rock that gives me peace.

Following the call of God can mean danger and persecution of varying degrees and of various types. There is no guarantee of safety in this life. But Jesus offers me peace despite the danger; He offers me peace and confidence in Him. I might step out in this world with a bit of trembling, but I have confidence in the One who goes with me. I have peace because my confidence or trust is not in myself—it's in Jesus. So I continue on my way believing that He who called me will make a way. Things might not turn out the way I want them to, but I have confidence and peace that they'll turn how God wants them to. God is my refuge, no matter what.

Amy Carmichael said, "The word comfort is from two Latin words meaning 'with' and 'strong'—He is with us to make us strong. Comfort is not a soft, weakening commiseration; it is true, strengthening love."[1] I think about the storm that the disciples faced while Jesus slept in the boat. They were so afraid, even though He who is comfort and peace was right there with them. They didn't find peace when the storm ended and the waters calmed, but they found peace in Jesus. Jesus is my peace. He is my comfort. He is my strengthening love. His love strengthens me when I'm scared or weak. He makes me strong. I take great comfort—great strengthening love—knowing that He is always with me.

Why do I need this peace? I'm a missionary kid that lives in Libya. It's not exactly the easiest place to be. But truthfully I need peace like everyone else on the planet because the enemy of our souls is making this world kind of crazy. As I take a stand for Jesus, the enemy will push against me. I need the peace and comfort of Jesus as I pursue His glory among the unreached. Jesus is my shield for battle and my peace in the storm. He is my confidence in the uncertain and blurry, and my rest in life and in death. Jesus is the Rock I stand on that can never be shaken. He is Who I walk in and stand on. He is my peace.

[1] Carmichael, Amy. *Kohila: The Making of an Indian Nurse.* CLC Ministries, July 2002.

Abide in Him

Is there anything in your life right now that is not peaceful? How does it make you feel?

Is there something happening in this nation or in the world that makes you nervous or fearful? How does that make you feel?

Joy wrote: "Still I know that I stand on a Rock that can never be shaken because my peace is not based on circumstances, people, or places, but on Jesus." There is freedom in knowing that peace does not come from what is happening around us. His love strengthens you when you feel scared or weak. He makes you strong.

Take a few minutes and talk with Jesus. Tell Him about the circumstances in your life or in the world that are not peaceful. Then ask Him to take their place. Ask for a peace not based on circumstances happening in your life, but based on Jesus. May His love bring strength and comfort into your life.

Write out this Scripture and put it in an area you can easily see everyday: "Fear not, for I am with you; be not dismayed, for I am your God. I will strengthen you, yes, I will help you, I will uphold you with My righteous right hand." (Isaiah 41:10)

SONGS FOR ABIDING:
"Hope's Anthem" (William Matthews, Bethel); "Lion and the Lamb" (Big Daddy Weave); "Tremble" (Mosaic MSC); "Prince of Peace" (Hillsong)

WHEN I AM SCARED, JESUS HELPS ME BY

Speaking to my heart and giving me parents that I can go to.

HANNA
North Africa
Age 12

> "*I need the peace and comfort of Jesus as I pursue His glory among the unreached.*"

DAY 19

It Takes a Village
Ecclesiastes 4; Psalm 104; Mark 6; 1 Corinthians 12

The church we attend in Libya is not a church we would choose if we were in America. It's quite different from what my family is used to, but we believe that meeting together in worship as believers is important. Especially when there are so few believers in this country. To be the body of Christ is a testimony to God's grace and love.

The few local believers here are the beginning of God's church in this country. They are the start of what God is doing here. But in order for this country in full to hear the gospel, it will take all hands on deck. It will take missionaries and the local church working together to see it happen. Our team must partner with local believers and with other missionaries to see Jesus exalted. We must lift up Jesus together, and not ourselves or our agendas.

We are stronger and more effective together in both practical and spiritual ways. In the practical, two are better than one. As we go visit homes together, maybe my friend's Arabic is better than mine. As she shares the gospel, I pray for wisdom and strength for her and for a revelation of Jesus for our hosts. In spiritual ways, we have the encouragement of knowing that we're not alone in this work and that other Christians here believe that Jesus will be glorified in Libya. We have the understanding that God called all of us here at this moment in time for His purpose.

Our work in partnership happens because we know it will require the whole church to take the whole gospel to the whole world. I want my small part of it to be about the work, not about myself. I'm not here because of who I am. I'm here because of Jesus. I want the work to proclaim who Jesus is, not who I am. The followers of Jesus in this country are here for the same reason. It's not about them; it's about Jesus. That motivation binds us together so that even our small differences don't break us apart.

The harvest will not happen if I am not willing to work with others, if my family and my team are not willing to work with other missionaries and the local church. We must be willing to go out in the heat of day to visit neighbors at home. We have to push through when it's hard, uncomfortable, and dangerous. We need to keep preparing the rocky soil even when we don't see the rain. I pray for rain. I pray for good soil. I pray for the harvest. I pray for the day that those who sow and those who reap will rejoice together, but until that day, we keep on planting seeds everywhere. This is not a weight we can carry on our own. It would take much longer for our small team to push and pull our way through it.

We are not the first ones in North Africa to do this kind of work. Many came before us. But those who start working early in the morning joined by those who start at noon joined by those who start near the day's end, we are all partnered for the harvest. We can't do it alone—someone breaks up the ground, someone drops the seeds, many come to water them, and others help them grow. This is not a race to see how far I can go alone, but to see how far we can relay together, working as a giant team.

IT TAKES A VILLAGE

Abide in Him

Do you enjoy working on a team, or do you like doing tasks on your own?

When working with a team on a project, why is it important to do your part? Write down a time (or more than one) when you used your gifts to glorify God through teamwork.

When it comes to sharing the gospel or being part of a church, do you believe that you're doing your part? Are you doing it for Jesus?

Take a few minutes and pray that you would work to do your part in this world, even if it's something you might not want to do or if it makes you feel uncomfortable. You might be the first person to ignite a passion in others to work together so the lost can know Jesus as their personal Savior!

SONGS FOR ABIDING:
"Break Every Chain" (Tasha Cobbs); "Be Enthroned" (Jeremy Riddle, Bethel); "Commission My Soul" (Citipointe Live)

I WOULD WANT KIDS COMING TO THE MISSION FIELD TO KNOW

That they should be willing to learn the new language—
and speak English with me, of course.

PAXTON
Middle East
Age 8

LIVE DEAD LIFE

"The harvest will not happen if I am not willing to work with others..."

DAY 20

Together
Proverbs 11; Psalm 133; Mark 9; 1 Peter 3

Last fall we had a thanksgiving service at the church my family attends. The congregation brought their offerings and laid them at the altar at the beginning of service. There were squawking turkeys all tied up, a goat lying on the floor, and chickens eager to break free over the course of the two and a half hour service. When the service finished, the animals were auctioned off as a fundraiser for the church. Now, I think all loud and smelly animals belong outside, but as a partner in the work to reach the lost (and as a kid with no say in the matter), I had to overlook the desire for my own comfort in order to see the big picture. I kept my thoughts to myself so our church could raise money and my arms at my side so as to not accidentally bid on a turkey.

Partnership is hard but beautiful. Partnership is a relationship, and like so many relationships in life, partnerships will have off-days. But also like so many relationships in life, partnerships will have blissful days. A partnership is like a friendship in which we must have a "we're in this together, so let's fight through it" mentality. In partnership, there is an equality in which no one has the upper hand or is superior over another. There is one Master and one goal—Him glorified. In partnership is great strength—there is someone to lift me up to Jesus when I'm down and vice versa.

My favorite thing about partnership is that it reveals the creativity of God through the cultures that cross borders to work together. There are so many backgrounds represented but there is one thing we have in common, one thing that holds us together—Jesus. God provides the grace to work, live, and love together because we love Jesus first. We find unity in our diversity as the love of Christ flows between us. We're all very different with our own sets of talents and flaws, but our differences don't hinder unity. Instead, they make our unity stronger because we complement and balance each other. My friend makes up for something that I'm not good at, and we learn from each other as we follow the example of Christ together.

Paul and the Philippian church are a good example of partnership. Once the church was planted in Philippi, it helped Paul move on to plant more churches. Through the joy of partnership, they encouraged each other and worked together. They had a relationship. The Philippians helped Paul in both practical and spiritual ways—they visited Paul in prison, supported him financially, showed concern for him, and lifted him up in prayer. The partnership brought both Paul and the Philippians joy. They encouraged one another and built each other up while working together in the practical and spiritual parts of life.

How cool would it be to see such a joy-filled, life-changing church planting work come from the partnership between the Libyan church and missionaries—a partnership in which we rejoice together in the victories and lift each other up through all the trials! I look forward to the day where there is a thriving local church in Libya that sends out its own Libyan missionaries to share the gospel in other parts of the world.

I don't know that I'm perfect at the partnership thing—it's sort of still new to me—but I really want to work in cooperation and not insist on my own way. I know I need to work on that humility and service part of me. I need a love for partnership that is stronger than a love for myself because I know every believer in the city needs to work together to see Jesus exalted here. I know there is strength in numbers, and as partners with the existing church as the body of Christ with the same mission, we will see the church grow together.

TOGETHER

Abide in Him

Why is partnership important? What is the point of partnership?

Think about your church and your community. Are you currently praying or serving side by side with others in sharing the love of Jesus?

Think of a friend with whom you can pray and brainstorm ideas on how to tell your peers about Jesus.

SONGS FOR ABIDING:
"Sons and Daughters" (North Point Inside Out); "Overcome" (Elevation Worship); "Simple Pursuit" (Passion, Melodie Malone)

I THINK FACING SAD AND BAD THINGS ON THE FIELD IS WORTH IT BECAUSE

It makes me stronger in Christ and helps me focus more on God if I trust in Him. When I first heard that I was going to another country, I was happy and sad. I was happy because I would get to see new things and travel on an airplane. I was sad because I would have to leave my family and friends.

When I'm sad or mad that I'm not with my family in America, I pray and ask God to help me think of all the wonderful things I've been able to do. It hasn't always been easy, but God is faithful and helps me through the hard times. When you trust God, He will help you through the hard times.

KAYLA
Egypt
Age 12

"My favorite thing about partnership is that it reveals the creativity of God..."

Apostle

APOSTOLIC FUNCTION
TEAM
PARTNERSHIP
PIONEERING

With time and some life experience, my understanding of these values has grown. Below are my thoughts now on what these values mean. Take a few minutes to reflect on the definitions you wrote earlier and consider if you might improve on them.

APOSTOLIC FUNCTION:

Apostolic function is God's command to go into all the world to preach the gospel and then the end will come (Math. 24:14). It's a command for all of us, and God invites us to share His passion to see the world reached. That means doing something—no matter where you are. We all play a part, though all parts are not all the same. No matter what we do, it all goes towards making Jesus' name known.

I define apostolic function as:

―――――――――――――――――――――――――――――――――
―――――――――――――――――――――――――――――――――

PIONEERING:

I still can't help but picture a pioneer woman with a white bonnet on her head when I hear the word "pioneer." I've learned pioneering is not always picture perfect with pretty bonnets. It's not an easy task. Leaving a trail for those to follow can be lonely and difficult. If the unreached are going to hear about Jesus, we'll have to step out of comfort zones and go to hard places.

I define pioneering as:

―――――――――――――――――――――――――――――――――
―――――――――――――――――――――――――――――――――
―――――――――――――――――――――――――――――――――

TEAM:

I have learned how effective team can be in fellowship and working together.

I define team as:

PARTNERSHIP:

Partnership is not just when we each do our part along the way but when we do it together side by side. It's about choosing together, as the body of Christ, to build a strong foundation that will help those who come after us weather the storms ahead.

I define partnership as:

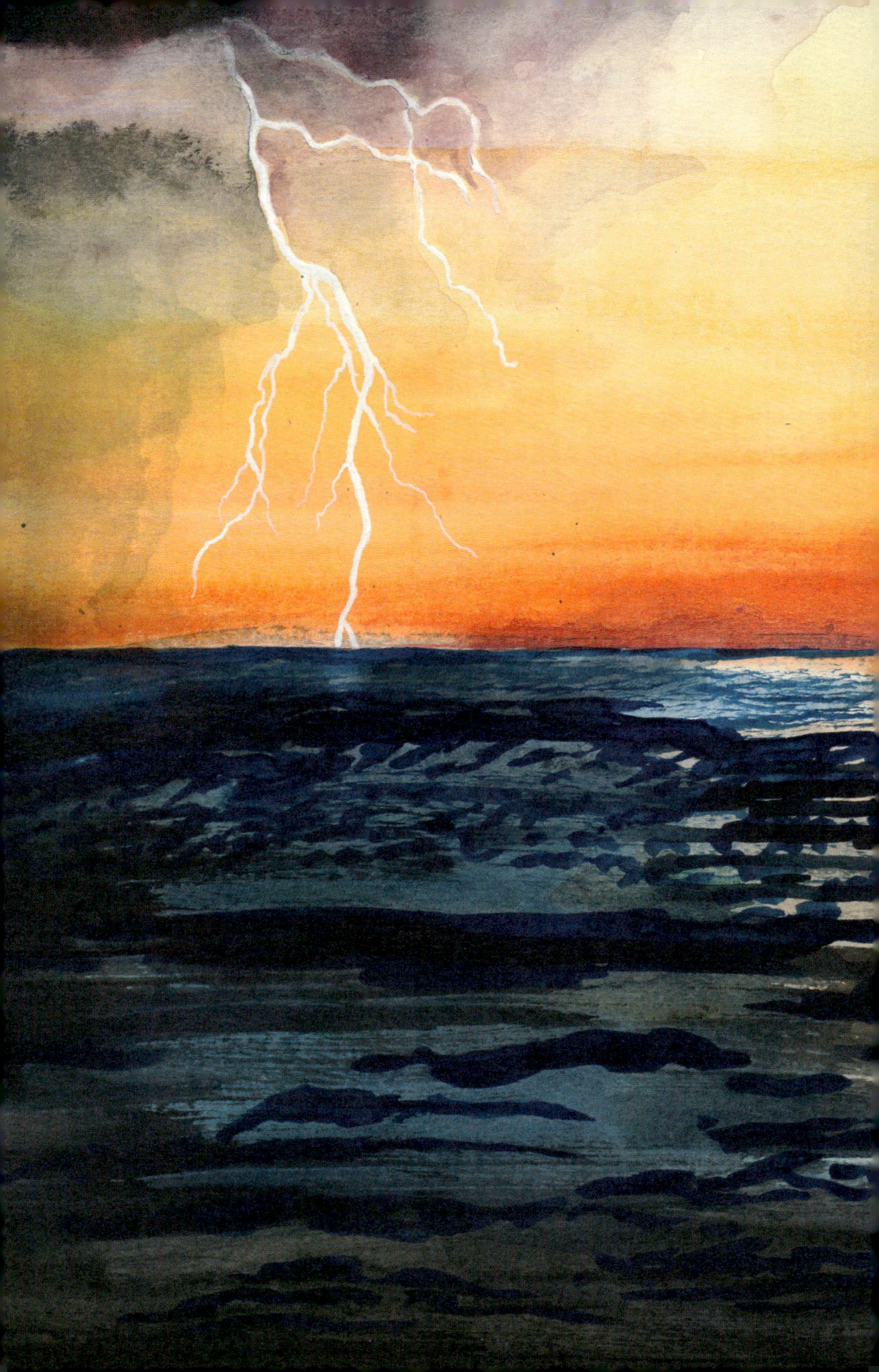

التخلي

Abandon

SACRIFICE
ACCOUNTABILITY
TRANSFORMATION
COMMUNITY

This last section includes my journal entries on our core value of Abandon. Abandon means to embrace suffering for Jesus' sake. It took a few years and a lot of experiences to better understand how these values work in daily life. Below are my thoughts on what I thought these words meant. Take a few minutes to write your own definitions.

SACRIFICE:

I never liked to think of the word sacrifice. It sounded too hard. It also felt far away from me. I usually imagined it to be about big things, and it was hard to think of sacrifices to make. Sacrifice was fear, not love, fear of what following Jesus might cost me, not love for Him.

I define sacrifice as:

ACCOUNTABILITY:

Being honest with other people, family, and friends. I pictured it as one-on-one with deep secrets. I knew we were supposed to have it, but it still sounded uncomfortable.

I define accountability as:

TRANSFORMATION:

I didn't know if this meant transformation in myself or in others.

I define transformation as:

COMMUNITY:

I didn't know if this meant the Arab community that lives around me or the body of Christ.

I define community as:

DAY 21

This Is Home

Daniel 3; Psalm 112; Luke 13; Acts 7

It began with: "Follow Me." So I followed Jesus. He led me to the cross He called me to die.

He invites me to come and die with Him. To die to myself and to sin. Which is not easy. It isn't something I do well. But it is something Christ asks me to do, so I keep fighting to do it. A daily death to self is the only way to follow. When I follow someone, it's mostly because I have no idea where I'm going. Daily I follow Jesus, and again, I might have no idea where He is leading me that day, but God is teaching me that He is there. Whether it's easy or hard that day, He is there. And I've discovered that where He is, there is joy, love, peace, and life.

For me, dying to myself and following Jesus daily can mean visiting neighbors when I don't want to, loving people I don't feel like loving, going where I am afraid to go, and doing things I am afraid to do. It often means letting go of my need for control and of my fear of what people think of me. Dying to myself frees me up to follow. I have to let go of me, so I can pick up my cross because I can't hold them both at the same time.

Jesus calls me to pick up my cross and follow Him. Follow Him where? Where is Christ going? Jesus is going to the same place that He went a couple thousand years ago—to the cross to die for the lost and the unreached. I've learned in my life that reached people have access to the message of Jesus—churches, Christian radio and bookstores, Christian neighbors, etc. The unreached have zero access to Jesus. They have never met a follower of Jesus. There is no missionary available to them. Zero churches, zero gospel witness.

My family is the first family that our church denomination has sent to Libya. The city where we live has two million people, and of those two million people, we personally know three local believers. Just three. Fighting is regular here, and it isn't safe to travel around much of the country. This is quite literally where no one else wants to go—except Jesus—and that is why we're here.

I love the quote from John Keith Falconer: "I have but one candle of life to burn, and I would rather burn it out in a land filled with darkness than in a land flooded with light." Some people think we're brave to live here; others think we're stupid. I know my family isn't the first to be here, or even the second, but we're here now. Jesus came when no one else would. He came as light in darkness. He came at a time and to a place that wasn't safe. He came and lived among us. He came and died for us. While it isn't easy, we're all called to do the same—to pick up our cross and follow Him. This is where He has led me. This is home.

Abide in Him

Why do you think it's important that Joy and her family die to themselves daily? What would their lives look like if they spent their time worrying about the present danger or difficulty of remaining in Libya?

Now consider what your life would look like if you daily died to self and sin. What does dying to self and following Jesus daily look like for you? Create a list with Jesus.

Dying to yourself means letting go of your need for control and allowing everything you do to glorify Jesus. Take a few minutes and search your heart. Do you die daily so you can freely follow Jesus? Pray that Jesus will take the highest place in your life.

SONGS FOR ABIDING:
"Once and for All" (Lauren Daigle); "Lead Me to the Cross" (Hillsong United); "The Wonderful Cross" (Chris Tomlin)

I LOVE BEING A MISSIONARY KID BECAUSE

We have the chance to travel around the world and experience amazing places. I also love it because I can develop relationships with cool people. I have a really good relationship with my friend Isabel. She is Portuguese but has lived in North Africa her whole life. She and I went to the French school together for four years. Even though I don't go to that school anymore, we still hang out on a regular basis.

E. F.
North Africa
Age 15

"Dying to myself frees me up to follow."

DAY 22

Cross Bearing

Deuteronomy 4; Psalm 1; Matthew 16; Romans 6

Symbols are important. Take the Declaration of Independence. Most days if I think about it, I just see it as a historical document. But it's more than that. It's a symbol of freedom and a dream for a new sovereign country.

There are symbols that are uplifting and represent victory, and there are symbols that are offensive and represent defeat. The cross can be viewed either way—as a symbol of victory or defeat, depending on the person you ask. Muslims here in Libya say that we shouldn't wear crosses. They see the cross as an image of the crusades. The cross is offensive to those who don't see understand the victory it represents. "For the message of the cross is foolishness to those who are perishing, but to us who are being saved it is the power of God" (1 Cor. 1:18). The cross is a symbol of death becoming life, of defeat becoming victory, of Jesus going from dead man to risen King. The cross brings victory for everyone!

I have to ask myself, "How will the unreached without access to the gospel hear about this cross of victory?" Someone must bring it to them. It's probably not in my best interest to carry a big, old, rugged cross down my street. No, the cross has to go from something only worn on the outside to something lived on the inside. I must pick up my cross daily inwardly and follow Jesus outwardly. He can then take me anywhere to do anything at anytime. I choose to live my life now for Jesus, the One who gave Himself for me. I choose to deny myself daily and say yes to Jesus. I choose to die that I might truly live and that others might also truly live. I choose to live dead not just for myself, but for those outside my door who have yet to hear. I choose to live with abandon, giving everything I have to follow Him.

This cross bearing, it is a daily battle between the old me and the new me. It's a battle between death and life. It's a fight in which I declare, "I am dead to sin and alive to God" (Rom. 6:11). Because how many times have I denied Him? I know it's been way more than three. So many times I say I'll go anywhere, but when He takes me in that direction, I get afraid and run away. I must stop denying Him and deny myself. Jesus gave me a good promise about that: "If anyone desires to come after Me, let him deny himself, and take up his cross, and follow Me. For whoever desires to save his life will lose it, but whoever loses his life for My sake will find it" (Matt. 16:24–25).

I follow Jesus, not only in the way He lived His life, but also in the way He died. I die daily for the love of Jesus and live in the love He has for me and for others. I deny myself to find hope in Him and give that same hope to others. I want everything I say and do to point to Jesus. I want everything I say and do to proclaim Jesus is Lord. He is King, not me.

There is the victory of the cross—dying to self, pride, and sin and turning back to God. It is when I fall and am buried that I rise up in the power of Jesus and bear fruit around me. When I live the crucified life, I find hope, forgiveness, and purpose. I find life in Jesus through the cross, the ultimate symbol of death to life.

CROSS BEARING

Abide in Him

What kind of person were you before Jesus?

What kind of person are you now because of Jesus?

Do you pick up your cross inwardly so it shows outwardly? When you are alone and no one is watching, does your life glorify Jesus?

Take a moment, and remember what you felt after accepting Jesus. Can you believe so many people have yet to experience that feeling? Pray that you would die to yourself so others can experience this freedom, too.

Perhaps through your example, others will want to know why you live your life differently. Imagine those around you worshipping Jesus and walking from darkness to light. It starts with you.

SONGS FOR ABIDING:
"At the Cross (Love Ran Red)" (Chris Tomlin, Passion); "Mighty Cross" (Elevation); "My Victory" (Passion, Crowder); "Found in You" (Vertical Church Band)

LIVING IN MY COUNTRY IS DIFFICULT BECAUSE

There are many high buildings and so much traffic.

HANNA
North Africa
Age 12

LIVE DEAD LIFE

"I must pick up my cross daily inwardly and follow Jesus outwardly."

DAY 23

No Risk Is Too Great

. Deuteronomy 26; Psalm 96; Luke 14; 1 Corinthians 13

There are certainly much nicer, easier, prettier, and more comfortable places to live than this city outside my door. I wouldn't mind living someplace where I could go to a church youth group, where I could go outside without covering my head, or where I could count on the electricity to stay on the whole day. It might be nice to live in a country that doesn't have so much conflict. But here we are, and it's good.

Rather than wish for a home with less risk and more comforts, I accept and follow God's plan for my life and find myself happy where He's placed my family. I willingly follow Him rather than draw lines in the sand of where I won't go and what I won't do. We go because, despite the risks, we know our God has a plan. We go because Jesus is worthy. He is worthy of my praise and the praise of the unreached I live among. No matter the cost, Jesus deserves all glory.

Risk is the possibility of harm coming to something or someone we value. What I value are things like money, family and friends, my stuff, and myself. Which makes me wonder—what does risk mean to God, what does He value? What the world values and what God values are often very different. First Corinthians 3:19 says, "For the wisdom of this world is foolishness in God's sight." Many of the things I value aren't bad in themselves, but it's the way or the amount I value them that can lead to harm or hurt should I lose them. I take a risk of being empty-handed when I value things in my life more than I value God.

I set aside what I value to take the risk for God because Jesus is worth it. He receives all the glory when I choose to proclaim Him in the middle of my circumstances, good or bad. This is about abandon. I won't sit and count the cost and keep a little for myself. I want to be all in. I want to be Mary and pour extravagant worship like oil on the feet of Jesus. I don't want to be Judas in the background criticizing it. I am willing to take the risk of handing over everything I value to possible harm, all for love. Here

I am saying I want to live like I'm dying and make what I do count, to proclaim with my words and with my life that Jesus is worth living and dying for.

There are days I ask myself, "Does God really need everything? Can He really use the little I have?" I often want to count the cost my way, to give God the leftovers, to offer the things that won't hurt or that I won't miss, to be less than extravagant in my worship. (I guess maybe I do have a little Judas in me.) Then I realized that I can't measure out what I want to give because I can't measure out the love of God. I can't take a handful of love and put it in a box. The love of God is immense and without end. His love never asks how far it has to go. The love of God reaches all. His love never portions itself out and saves for later. His love is without end; it's eternal. The love of God does not hide from its neighbors. His love is always available. So just as the love of God is always poured out, so I must pour myself out, so I must hand over what I value—my time, money, my popularity, my life.

In the Old Testament, the Israelites brought their first fruits, their best, as an offering to God. I will do the same, give the best I have to offer of my time, money, myself, my family. For the unreached to be reached, everyone must count the cost and submit our lives to the risk. The cost of following Jesus for many here in Libya could be death. If one Muslim in Libya becomes a disciple of Jesus, no matter what happens to me or my family, if that is what I really want to see, then what am I holding back for? I must sacrifice comfort for the unknown, uncomfortable land. Others must send those they love. We must give, even when it hurts. As we do this together, the people around me will be reached.

Abide in Him

Joy mentioned that "many of the things I value aren't bad in themselves but it's the way or the amount I value them that can lead to harm or hurt should I lose them." Make a list of things you value. Do you value any of those things more than God?

Pray about the list you just created. If you currently value other things more than God, pray deeply and sincerely that He would give you the grace to replace those things with Him.

Will you risk handing everything you value over for the gospel? Talk to Jesus about this. Let His love comfort you.

Do you currently give the best of your time to be a part of the lost coming to Jesus?

SONGS FOR ABIDING:
"Have It All" (Bethel); "Christ Is Enough" (Hillsong); "Frontiers (Vertical Church Band)

ONE THING JESUS HAS TAUGHT ME ABOUT MISSIONS IS

It isn't easy. Although being a missionary kid is amazing, it comes with difficulties like not being able to see your family back in the States when you want to. The fact that you probably won't see them for a few years can be hard and frustrating.

LOGAN
North Africa
Age 17

"*I set aside what I value to take the risk for God because Jesus is worth it.*"

DAY 24

Face the Danger
Jonah 3; Psalm 91; Matthew 24; 2 Corinthians 11

I live in a place that is…not entirely safe. But then I think about the story of Jonah, which at first I remember being a story about a fish that swallows a man because he disobeyed God's call. I learned later about why Jonah refused God's call to go to Nineveh. It was because Nineveh was dangerous. The people there were the enemy of Jonah's people. No one wanted to go there, except God. Sometimes I give the "anything but that" answer to God. Anywhere You want God, except there. Except that's not how it works, if I already committed to carry my cross. If I wait for the dangerous places, like Libya, to become stable and welcoming, well, I might be waiting for eternity.

There are many who say that my family is foolish to live here, that the risk is too great, that we should live somewhere safer, that God would never send us here. All of that would totally be true if security and safety were the greatest needs in life. But I know God called my family to this place, so we stay and work until He tells us otherwise. Life here is risky and hard, but Jesus is worth it. Besides, I don't think my life is too high a price to pay for a Muslim to come to Jesus. I believe my life is well spent if even one-in-a-million hears for the gospel for the first time.

I hear that others wait and wonder if the time is right to come here. I say the time to come is now! I have so many opportunities to sow seeds and share with people. True, not every person here is super welcoming, but the majority do welcome me with open arms and great excitement. I'd venture to say that when I meet someone here for the first time, I am probably the first Christian she has ever met in her life. The first one! That blows my mind. And as time goes by, I am less surprised that these people are open to the message of Jesus. The war and disorder in their world are starting to show the cracks in Islam. I feel honored to be here at this critical—even if dangerous—time in the country's history.

People ask if I feel safe here. "Safe" is a tricky word. I'm happy here. I'm content, thankful, and secure in Christ. I feel safe when I'm at the park playing with kids and visiting with women. I feel safe with all my Muslims friends and neighbors around me—they love us and we love them. Much of life is normal, even with fighting around us. I feel safe today, but in case something should happen to me tomorrow, I want to take every opportunity today. God knows what I need, and until my work here is done, I am untouchably covered by Jesus' blood. That doesn't mean I am looking for death, but my family and I follow and obey Jesus above all other concerns. Right now, that means here. I believe God is in control; therefore the risk is not too great. I can live for Jesus and die for others because Jesus already died and rose again. I don't think Satan wants me to go to the dangerous, difficult, unreached places. He would rather I stay home. Believing this, will I be afraid or will I be bold?

FACE THE DANGER

Abide in Him

What are your thoughts about living in a place that isn't safe? What does safe mean to you?

Joy mentioned that she was happy, content, thankful, and secure in Christ, despite her living situation. How can you apply this to your own life? Where do you find your contentment?

Has there been a time God asked you to do something, but fear stopped you?

Take a few minutes to talk to God about your answers to these questions. Perhaps you deal with fear and need courage to do things that are not easy. Perhaps you feel like you have it all, but you feel no contentment in your life. Regardless of what it might be, know that God hears you and He wants to complete you.

SONGS FOR ABIDING:
"You Make Me Brave" (Amanda Cook, Bethel); "Waiting Here for You" (Jesus Culture); "There Is a Cloud" (Elevation Worship

JESUS IS WORTH LIVING FOR BECAUSE

He died on the cross for us, and He loves us.

BENJAMIN
North Africa
Age 10

"I'm happy here. I'm content, thankful, and secure in Christ."

DAY 25

The See-Through Me Is Free

Proverbs 27; Psalm 90; Matthew 22; James 4

The older I get, the more freedom my parents give me. Sometimes I feel pretty independent. "I got this," I think. I know my goals, and I know how to reach them.

But I've discovered it doesn't always work out quite right if I'm left to my own devices—even if one of those devices is prayer. I need to remember freedom and strength for daily living comes from dependence on God and on others. It comes from transparency with God and with others. I can do more and grow stronger when I rely on God and those people He places around me, more than if I tried it all on my own. Independence is good for some things. Accountability is good for all things.

Accountability frees me. I need accountability. There is security in accountability. It keeps me safe. It can keep me from mistakes. It takes away worry. It helps me place my plans in God's hands. I thought accountability tied me up and took away my independence and the chance to make decision, but whenever I am dishonest or hide things, I feel like a wall goes up. I feel cut off from others. I feel less effective in my witness and walk with God. In that place, life becomes a lie and lying becomes exhausting. It holds me captive. But whenever I share what's happening in my life, when I confess what I'm thinking or feeling, there is no wall. The air is clear, and I feel like I can freely talk to my mom, my dad, my siblings and friends, and to Jesus.

Accountability is also about respect. I can give the gift of respect to my parents, to older team members, to our leaders, and to anyone in authority over me. I also need to give the gift of respect to those in authority with whom I disagree or simply find disagreeable. That is a hard gift to give sometimes. Sometimes I feel like they don't deserve my respect or submission, like they're wrong and I'm right. But when I make the choice to show respect (maybe with loads of grace), I honor them, and I honor Jesus.

There are some days when I think I'd rather do without any accountability, but then I remember that honesty keeps things real and clear. It helps me accomplish more because I'm not holding back or trying to hide something or trying to remember what to say or what not to say. Transparency turns my stumbling blocks into stepping stones so I can grow and help others to grow and lift Jesus higher. Transparency builds trust and helps me live and work better with others. Transparency builds relationships on foundations of love and trust. When I honor my family (or anyone) with honesty, it builds trust.

I have the freedom to choose—the choice to follow Jesus in accountability or lead myself. That choice decides everything after it: where I go, where I stay, who I am, who I am not. When I live a transparent life, I feel free and lightweight because I don't hold anything in that weighs me down. In a transparent life, God uses our weaknesses because He is glorified through our weaknesses. I have so much to learn from God through accountability, whether it's through my parents, siblings, friends, fellow team members, or leaders. And it's in accountability that I begin to resemble Jesus, a servant and ransom for many, where I set aside my wants for the greater good of His glory. I need accountability so that Jesus becomes greater and I become less.

Abide in Him

Is there anyone in your life that holds you accountable? Is there someone with whom you can be absolutely honest?

Do you feel captive, exhausted, or cut off from others because you haven't shared some things?

Accountability frees you and allows you to learn the importance of transparency. If you don't already have someone like this in your life, take a moment and ask God who a good accountability person might be for you.

If you have people with whom you can be transparent, do you openly share everything, and are you presently growing? Ask God what steps you might take to go deeper.

SONGS FOR ABIDING:
"You Know Me" (Steffany Gretzinger, Bethel Music); "Unstoppable Love" (Jesus Culture, Kim Walker-Smith); "The More I Seek You" (Kari Jobe)

JESUS IS WORTH DYING FOR BECAUSE

Most of you have probably heard that if we believe in Him, we will be in heaven for eternity with Him. What better place to go than heaven?

J. E.
North Africa
Age 17

> "When I honor my family (or anyone) with honesty, it builds trust."

DAY 26

Now That You Know
Proverbs 9; Psalm 145; Matthew 28; James 2

Sometimes I don't want to take responsibility. I'm not talking about not owning up to what I've done wrong, though I find that hard to do, too. I'm talking about stepping up and taking responsibility for a wrong or injustice I see happening in front of me. Sometimes I don't want to commit to that responsibility. I could hide behind the excuse of inexperience or youth, but the fact is, if I'm smart enough to recognize the problem or if my spirit is pricked over the problem, then I probably have some amount of ability to take on responsibility for what I've seen.

Taking responsibility is a step that I—and many Jesus followers—need to make. A full-out follower of Jesus, I need to respond to what He shows me and what He pricks my heart to do and follow Him to the answer. What will I do right now—not when I'm older, not when I feel more qualified, not when I have more to give, but right now. My choice to respond to a need becomes my responsibility. Will I see it through?

There is a responsibility that comes with what I know about Jesus. The gospel demands I do something with it. What will I do with the knowledge I have? I cannot hide it in a closet because there is no benefit—not to myself or to anyone else. I need to share it. I have a responsibility to share with others, to set myself aside, to follow Jesus outside my door. I am responsible for what I did for myself but also what I did for others, not for what I cherished for myself, but for what I lovingly and joyfully gave away. Jesus shared a parable about talents. In that parable He tells His listeners how much each person received and what he did the amount. I could be the one who received the larger amount or the smaller amount, but the amount matters less than my management of it. Until Jesus returns, I am responsible for what He puts in my hands and how I use it. I could choose to horde the message or I could choose to be responsible and take the message outside my door to my city. What will I do with it? Keep it to myself or share it with others? This is my daily choice—who do I live for, myself or Jesus?

Today there is a man walking in a neighborhood in America, and there is a Bedouin Arab woman walking in a desert in Libya, and they are both lost. They both need Jesus. While they have this in common, their situations are very different. The man in America has access to the gospel. There are churches, radio stations, Bibles, and Christians around him. The Bedouin woman has no access to the gospel. There is no church, missionary, or gospel witness. The One who can make a difference in their lives is the same—Jesus—and the ones with the responsibility are the same—His church. Jesus cares just as much about the Bedouin woman as He cares about the man in America. He will do whatever it takes for the lost to hear His Name, and His plan includes every believer. He calls everyone to the Great Commission everywhere. I will pray that a Christian will cross paths with this man in America to explain the gospel to him. At the same time, I will step outside my door and take responsibility for those I meet in Libya.

My teen years are the perfect opportunity. I have more time and energy now than I might have in a few years. I want to take responsibility for the message of Jesus and for the people around me. The time is now. There is no good reason to wait. My door is open, and Jesus calls me to follow Him through it.

Abide in Him

Joy's response as a follower of Jesus is her understanding of her responsibility in Libya. She is committed to praying for the lost in America and sharing the gospel with those in Libya. She decides daily to either live for herself or for Jesus. She wants to take responsibility to share the message of Jesus to those around her.

There is a responsibility to you knowing Jesus. What will your response be? Will you share the gospel in America or wherever you call home? Will you pray for Joy and other families living in places like Libya?

What stops you from sharing the gospel at home?

Imagine that God is sitting in a chair next to you. Turn to Him and tell Him how thankful you are that you heard the gospel. Thank Him for His grace and unconditional love. Share your heart and ask Him to help you live out your responsibility.

We are all in different places with the same mission: That all should hear the gospel. Ask God for a deeper burden to pray for other young people like you living in places like Libya. Pray that their commitment would encourage you to do the same right in your community, and share your commitment to encourage them to keep pressing on (#livedead).

SONGS FOR ABIDING:
"Great Are You Lord" (All Sons and Daughters); "Grace to Grace" (Hillsong Worship); "Albertine" (Brooke Fraser)

IF SOMETHING BAD HAPPENS TO MY FAMILY, I WILL BE OK BECAUSE

God is with us.

DAVID & SARA
North Africa
Age 10 & 9

LIVE DEAD LIFE

"My door is open, and Jesus calls me to follow Him through it."

DAY 27

Come Sit With Us

1 Kings 17; Psalm 72; Luke 17; Acts 8

There are countless needs in the world: famine, poverty, brokenness, and war. I could easily be overwhelmed by it all. I am the hands and feet of Jesus, but I have no idea where to start. I can't rate pain. I can't rate need. I can only ask to see through God's eyes with His heart and ask where He is going today and then follow Him. Jesus is the One who touched lepers, opened blind eyes, and raised the dead. Jesus transformed lives. For those who believed He was the Messiah, He transformed hearts, and I believe that same Jesus is available to the unreached of Libya today. He desires to see their hearts transformed.

There are nearly six million unreached people in Libya. The need for heart transformation is great, and transformation happens when the need meets Jesus. How do I introduce the two? Well, I start with one person and point to Jesus. The search for hearts in need of transformation is not hard here, and life in general here makes for many easy conversations. So many Libyans feel hopeless. On a walk, I can stop and talk to the lady across the street. I can accept an invitation to a picnic or tea. I can share the hope and peace I have in Jesus. I can pray for personal encounters with Him. I can stop and pray for the sick to be healed as I pass by them. "Just come sit with us," they might say, and I can happily sit with them.

The Ethiopian eunuch in Acts 8 had a heart need like my Libyan neighbors do, and he didn't have the answer either. God called Philip to go meet him. He found the official reading from the book of Isaiah and asked, "Do you understand what you're reading?" The Ethiopian replied, "How can I unless someone explains it to me?" So he invited Philip to sit with him, and Philip preached Jesus to him. God prepared a way for Philip to share and for the Ethiopian to hear. In the end, the Ethiopian proclaimed Jesus Christ as the Son of God and was baptized on the spot! Before talking to Philip, he had no idea who Isaiah was prophesying about or what that one Person meant for his life. Similar conversations take place here in Libya every day—but we need more of them! Libyans need someone to sit with them and explain who Jesus is and what He means for their lives. They need the truth to meet their need!

I pray and believe for the Holy Spirit's work of transformation in the lives of my neighbors, friends, and complete strangers here. I believe when they meet Jesus and supernaturally see the look of love in His eyes, when they hear and accept the truth of the gospel, when they sense His healing of their terminal diseases, they will say yes to His answer, and in an instant He will transform them. This transformation to a new person, to a heart transformed, is a new life lived for Jesus.

Transformation is a new road to a new life with a new purpose, and I'm just here as a road sign to it, to Him. Once I pointed only to myself, which would be like a wrong way sign, but now I point to Jesus, to the answer. I point to the Creator, because with one touch, Jesus creates new lives. The lame walk, the blind see, and the dead come to life. Sometimes the healing of a physical need opens the way for a person to listen to the story that meets their greatest need. The physical needs in life can't be ignored. There are many poor people and sick people in this world, so however I can help them in the physical, I will always point to the spiritual. I cannot be the answer to their every physical need, but I can always share the answer to their every spiritual need. The need will not be met if they do not meet Jesus, and I choose to share the Bread of Life and the Living Water right outside my door.

Abide in Him

What are needs around the world that seem too enormous, perhaps even impossible, to fix all by yourself?

Meeting a need in this world can feel overwhelming, but there is something you can do from right where you are. You can pray for the one in need to have an encounter with Jesus and experience life transformation.

Spend some time praying for the lost. Pray for a person living in a war-stricken area, a person living in poverty, and/or a person without access to the gospel. Pray that a believer would sit down with each of them and share the truth about Jesus. Pray that each one would receive a Bible and have the opportunity to hear about Jesus.

Now consider the lost in your community and pray the same prayers.

Joy wrote, "I cannot be the answer to their every physical need, but I can always share the answer to their every spiritual need." What will your response be to the spiritual needs of others? Write it down.

SONGS FOR ABIDING:
"All Things New" (Elevation Worship); "You Are My Passion" (Jesus Culture); "Miracles" (Jesus Culture)

SOMETHING THAT SCARES ME IS

Thinking about if the army ever started fighting close to our house or started searching for us.

ELLA GRACE
North Africa
Age 12

> *"I pray and believe for the Holy Spirit's work of transformation in the lives of my neighbors, friends, and complete strangers here."*

DAY 28

The Little Red Heart
Ruth 1; Psalm 136; Matthew 18; 1 John 4

That red heart is my go-to emoji in text messages. It's also the quick tap to show my love on social media. I love a good Valentine's Day card that has a nice, symmetrical, cute, red heart. That red heart makes love easy to express. It makes it easy to express an emotion, feeling, or agreement toward a person, topic, idea, or whatever. That red heart, synonymous with love, kind of waters down love though. It makes it easy, makes it safe.

Christians, disciple-makers, children of God only love "because [God] first loved us" (1 John 4:19). I only love because God loved me first. I only know love because I see it in Him first. Christ loved me by coming and doing something that no one else would do. I hear the phrase "God is love" a lot, and it is absolutely true. But I have to remember not to cram God into my little "red heart" definition of love because love came to earth, lived and died. Love died. Died for me! Love feels pain. Christ endured the cross, endured the pain and torture so that I could be whole.

First Corinthians 13 says this about love: "Love is patient, love is kind. It does not envy, it does not boast, it is not proud. It does not dishonor others, it is not self-seeking, it is not easily angered, and it keeps no record of wrongs. Love does not delight in evil but rejoices with the truth. It always protects, always trusts, always hopes, and always perseveres." Love does a lot. It does more than just "like" a few photos on Instagram. Love actually sounds a lot like daily dying. It sounds a lot like Jesus. And it sounds really hard. Maybe even painful.

This love, the love of the cross, takes the risk. This love meets me right where I am, in the good and the bad. It doesn't always tell me that it's going to be okay, but it definitely stays with me, to do in the moment what words cannot—just love me. This love of the cross casts out fear. It makes the sacrifice; it dies for me and for those in my city. This love of the cross is the way I love and live as I pick up my cross and follow Jesus. Do I trust God enough to love the way that Christ loved me? God calls me today to truly love, to walk in the love of the cross.

So often I define love for myself. I love others because of what they've done for me. But that's selfish love, not selfless love, not the selfless love of the cross that gives all unconditionally. It's hard to love some people. There are people I might not agree with or I might not see eye to eye with, but I can still love them. I might not like what a friend does or says, but I can still love, serve, respect, and honor her. I discovered in these situations and relationships that love is a risk, but I also see the worth and I can invest the love because that is what Jesus did for me. He died on the cross, and He said I was worth it.

The unreached people surrounding me are worth it, too, and I daily learn to the love people that, sometimes, don't want to make it easy on me. I and my family and our team, we give and love long and hard, over and over, day after day, but without much fruit in return. These people still seem as hard as they were on day one. But this love of the cross is for them. Day in and day out, I do it again, loving them one day after another. When I feel like I'm dizzy from going in circles, I return to the love of the cross. He fills me to overflowing so I can once again pour out, with no guarantee of return. I do it because this love, the love of Jesus, is not for me to keep, it's for me to give away. It's for me to share with those who have yet to hear.

There are many days I wish I knew how many circles I have to make around someone before she says, "Yes," or "Get lost," for good. I wish this love thing had a formula to it. "How many times do I have to forgive?" Peter asked, holding up seven fingers. Jesus looked at him and multiplied it—seventy times seven or "don't keep a count." Love can be a lot of work, with no formula. There are no words, books, or ideas that I can just toss together. Love is a life, but it's a life that I don't have to do alone. Love doesn't come from me. Love is all Jesus. He is my example to follow daily. So I live in Jesus, the love of the cross. I love in all the little ways of my life as I live in the huge love of the cross.

Abide in Him

What does "God is love" mean to you? Do you believe that this love is enough?

What is your definition of love? What does the word "love" mean to you?

Is there someone in your life that you have a difficult time loving? Are you walking and living with the love of the cross?

Search your heart right now. Ask God to help you truly love with the love of the cross. Ask Him to help you love those who hurt you in the past and will hurt you in the future.

SONGS FOR ABIDING:
"Elohim" (Hillsong Worship); "Steady Heart" (Steffany Gretzinger); "When I Lost My Heart to You" (Hillsong United)

WHEN I AM SCARED, JESUS HELPS ME BY

By His Word.

PAXTON
Middle East
Age 8

LIVE DEAD LIFE

> "*I love in all the little ways of my life as I live in the huge love of the cross.*"

DAY 29

Dancing Required
2 Samuel 6; Psalm 149; Mark 2; Acts 2

I don't dance. I mean, I would if I could, but I really can't. So I politely said no. But the woman who invited us insisted: "Yes."

Oh, the horror I felt as she dragged us to the dance floor at a wedding with one hundred pairs of eyes staring straight at us. Now would be the time to disappear, for the floor to open and suck me in. But it didn't.

"Jesus, please help me."

It was just another day living among these beautiful, passionate, strong, funny people.

Community is essential if we are to survive and thrive here. I am so thankful for the community we have. They make us feel like family. In our community we have people of peace (Luke 10:6) who stand on our behalf. They go with us to help with paperwork and drive across town just to find us cooking gas. They protect and care about us. We keep our eyes open for new people of peace God brings on our way. They might be people of influence, people who are a key part of the local community. They might be able to help me with language and teach me about their culture. They're not usually hard to find because people here are fun and easy to laugh with. They are open and willing to help.

Now, my family could choose to just live near them, next to them, sharing our message as we pass by, but not sharing our lives by living among them. The problem with that is that's not the example Jesus left us. Jesus spent time around tables filled with food sharing stories. He spent time teaching, encouraging, and sometimes rebuking. He met the needs of the people. He walked in their dust. The people knew there was something different about Him. They sought Him out and found Him—and He never ran and hid. Instead, He fed them, healed them, and defended them.

I'm not Jesus—not even close. I could never live among others and love them so perfectly on my own. But with Jesus, I can. I can step outside my door and visit their homes and drink tea with them. I can talk about life, share hope, listen to stories, and tell mine. I can commit to this community. I can be present with my friends. I can be family when they feel alone or abandoned. Maybe they'll notice something different about me. Maybe they'll see Jesus in my life and His hope in my words, and they will want to know about the One that I pray I will never stop talking about. I want them to wonder what is so different about Jesus, that they would be unable to find any comparison between Muhammad their prophet and Jesus the Son of God.

Our team doesn't just share our message; we share our lives. Community gives us a place to reach our neighbors with the gospel. As we share our lives and hearts with them, they see how we live the message of the good news. Living in community gives us the platform to speak the gospel; it doesn't take the place of sharing the gospel. It gives our friends the chance to see Jesus in everything we do. I know that not every Libyan will be my best friend. I have to be intentional about with whom I spend my time because I don't have unlimited time. I pray for God to direct my path as well as the paths of the people I need to meet. People here want relationship. They want to spend time together, so when I sense that God has brought a specific person my way, I take the time to form a friendship with her.

I so want my family and our team to become more than just those crazy Americans to my Libyan friends and neighbors. I want to become the people who are different—not just kind and caring for a good cause—but those who can't stop talking about Jesus. So I will intentionally sacrifice and spend time with my community to share life with them so I can share Jesus with them—even if I have to dance to do it.

Abide in Him

What impression do you think you leave with people? Do you leave the impression that you're kind, compassionate, or loving? Write down a few things that you believe people think of you.

Do you believe people leave you undoubtedly knowing that you are passionate about Jesus? If yes, why?

You're in a conversation, and someone asks you, "Why are you a Christian?" What is your answer?

One way to share Jesus is to look for opportunities to invite Him into your conversations every day. Take some time to pray that you will be prepared and willing to talk about Jesus. Pray that through your conversations, others will know that you love Jesus and will be interested in knowing more.

SONGS FOR ABIDING:
"We Dance" (Steffany Gretzinger, Bethel); "God's Great Dance Floor" (Chris Tomlin); "Bound for Glory" (Vertical Church Band)

I WOULD WANT KIDS COMING TO THE MISSION FIELD TO KNOW

There are so many kids in the Middle East and other places that need Jesus, and kids can share and get close to other kids way better than an adult can.

ABRAM
North Africa
Age 13

LIVE DEAD LIFE

> "I am so thankful for the community we have."

DAY 30

I Seek Approval
Daniel 6; Psalm 16; Luke 12; Acts 5

Fear pricks me in many different ways. In the dark when I can't see. At the times I don't know what to do. When I don't know what's going to happen next. If I think that I or someone I love will get hurt. Some of my fears are silly, like my fear of the bats that live upstairs in our storage room. Fear is natural response to physical danger. Fight or flight? It can also be an irrational response to something I believe might be dangerous. All of my fears have one thing in common—me. I'm afraid of what could happen to me. I'm afraid of what people will think of me. I'm afraid I'm not enough—which of any fear is probably the most true because no matter what I think of myself, I'm not enough. Thankfully, Jesus is.

Fear is something that needs to be let in. I'm not an innocent victim of fear if I let it in and let it control me. It's easy to have a victim mentality. I can quickly say, "I couldn't help it." Like I was unable to fight it. But I can fight it with Jesus. Covered by the blood of Jesus, I can fight back fear.

So how do I respond to fear? Do I hold on to it and let it replay over and over in my head? Or do I give it to Jesus? Fear comes when I think it's all up to me, when I think I have to make that fight or flight decision, instead of depending on God who holds and sees my problems way better than I every could. Elisabeth Elliot wrote, "Fear arises when we imagine that everything depends on us."[2] Deuteronomy 33:27 says, "The eternal God is your refuge, and underneath are the everlasting arms." Surrendering my fears gives me something so much better—faith in God my refuge. When I'm afraid, I can trust in Jesus. It might not mean that everything is going to be okay, but I can trust Him to carry me through. God is trustworthy.

One of my biggest fears is the fear of what others think. Often I try to conform to what others want or think so I fit in. But I'm not the same, and I'm not meant to be the same. What I do or what I'm meant to do is not the same as what my friend does. Who I am is not the same as who she is. I think of friends back home. We share many things in common—we are all children of God, dearly loved by Him and made to glorify Him. But we're not the same person on the same path. We each have our gifts, and I need to learn to give my best and not see myself as a second rate somebody else.

I want to be free of this fear. I want to live for the one opinion that really matters: God's. What I need to do is step out and follow Jesus, and while I don't do it for this reason, I think others may very well join me if I do. No matter if others laugh or if I seem a little crazy, I will step outside my door and follow Jesus without fear today. I will live free of this fear. Having a few people laugh at me because I'm a Christian is a mild form of suffering, even if it does hurt. No one likes being made fun of or left feeling stupid. But what if in those moments I left rejoicing? The disciples faced something like this. In Acts the Pharisees told them to stop talking about Jesus. The disciples said no and they were beaten for it. They left rejoicing though because they were counted worthy to suffer for the name of Jesus. What if I just wasn't afraid of what someone thinks because I'm so consumed with Jesus? What if I followed Him and never looked back to hear what they had to say? What if I wasn't afraid to stand and speak up? What if I stopped seeking the crowd's approval? I don't need it because I don't live for them. I live for Jesus.

---

[2] Elisabeth Elliot, *The Music of His Promises: Listening to God with Love, Trust, and Obedience*, Fleming H. Revell Company, 2004.

I SEEK APPROVAL

Abide in Him

What are some of you biggest fears? Describe them.

How do you handle your fears? Do you share them with Jesus or with others, or do you keep them to yourself?

Take a look at your list of fears. Did you know that you don't have to hold on to them? Read through the list out loud, and as you do, imagine handing them to God. Pray against those fears, and declare that God is your refuge. After you finish praying through each one, cross it out and put today's date next to it.

Know that you are no longer a slave to fear. You are a child of God.

SONGS FOR ABIDING:
"Satisfied in You (Psalm 42)" (The Sing Team); "No Longer Slaves" (Jonathan David Helser, Melissa Helser, Bethel Music); "Not Today" (Hillsong United)

I THINK FACING SAD AND BAD THINGS ON THE FIELD IS WORTH IT BECAUSE

You learn to turn to God in those hard times. Perhaps you've heard it said that iron is made strong through fire, but there's more than just sticking iron in the fire. The iron must be cared for, shaped, and forged in the fire, or it'll just be consumed and burned. A blacksmith uses the fire to mold and shape the iron and to strengthen it. We face hardship no matter what, but on the field, most of the time you have nowhere to go but back to God. That is what fire is supposed to do—strengthen you so that God may use you, not harden you into twisted steel, bent, useless, stubborn, scorched, and broken.

LUKE
Egypt
Age 18

"Covered by the blood of Jesus, I can fight back fear."

Abandon

SACRIFICE
ACCOUNTABILITY
TRANSFORMATION
COMMUNITY

With time and some life experience, my understanding of these values has grown. Below are my thoughts now on what these values mean. Take a few minutes to reflect on the definitions you wrote earlier and consider if you might improve on them.

SACRIFICE:

When I choose to obey and make a sacrifice, it's an open door to the next step of following Jesus.

I define sacrifice as:

ACCOUNTABILITY:

Accountability doesn't have to be an awkward burden. It can bring refreshing. I now see accountability as something we do together. Some of our greatest challenges are with each other and we need to bring those weaknesses to Jesus together.

I define accountability as:

TRANSFORMATION:

This happens daily in me and in those who are being saved, as Jesus makes us more like Himself.

I define transformation as:

COMMUNITY:

I found community. We share life with them and point them to where our hope and peace comes from—Jesus.

I define community as:

A PRAYER

As I finished this journal, I wrote a prayer to Jesus for myself and for you. You can pray this prayer out loud today, or use it as a starting point for your own prayer of commitment to Jesus.

DEAR JESUS,

We come before You and offer You our willing hearts. You don't need us, yet You want us. You invite us to follow You, and this invitation is more than we could ever dream or imagine.

Too often fear holds us back from stepping outside our doors into the unknown, yet we believe that You prepare the way for each of us. Help us to trust You, to lean on You as our Rock, and to follow You as our Risen Master.

Help us to abandon everything to You because You are worthy of it all. You are worthy of our lives. You are worthy of the praise and love of every tribe and nation on earth. Give us Your heart. Make our hearts overflow for every people. Give us Your eyes to see the world.

As we walk with You daily, show us what You see in the journey. Help us to see the important things You ask us to do, not as a duty, but as an invitation to relationship. We don't want to miss out on what You have planned for us, wherever that might be.

Lord, we recognize not only our need for You, but also for each other. We want to follow Your commands and seek You together. You've chosen us to be Your disciples. As You send us out, may we never keep the good news to ourselves. May we not stay silent because we fear the cost of speaking out. By Your own perfect example and love, help us to pick up our crosses and lay everything else at Your feet.

Today we choose to step outside our doors and follow You.

Amen.